Jacobins
AND Utopians

Frank M. Covey, Jr.

Loyola Lectures in Political Analysis

Thomas S. Engeman

General Editor

Our late colleague Richard S. Hartigan founded the Frank M. Covey, Jr., Lectures in Political Analysis to provide a continuing forum for the reanimation of political philosophy. The lectures are not narrowly constrained by a single topic nor do they favor a particular perspective. Their sole aim is to foster serious theoretical inquiry, with the expectation that this effort will contribute in essential ways to both human knowledge and political justice.

Jacobins

AND *Utopians*

The Political Theory of Fundamental Moral Reform

George Klosko

UNIVERSITY OF NOTRE DAME PRESS
Notre Dame, Indiana

Manufactured in the United States of America

Library of Congress Cataloging-in-Publication Data
Klosko, George.
Jacobins and utopians : the political theory of fundamental moral
reform / George Klosko.
p.   cm. — (Frank M. Covey, Jr. Loyola lectures in political analysis)
Includes bibliographical references and index.
ISBN 0-268-03257-2 (cloth : alk. paper)
ISBN 0-268-03258-0 (pbk. : alk. paper)
1. Revolutions.   2. Political science — History.   3. Social ethics.
4. Social reformers.   5. Power (Social sciences)   I. Title.   II. Series.

JC491 .K54 2003
321'.07 — dc21

2002013373

∞ *This book is printed on acid-free paper.*

To the memory of

Emanuel Klosko

The Memory of the Righteous Is a Blessing.

Contents

Nous voulons, en un mot, remplir les voeux de la nature,
accomplir les destins de l'humanité, tenir les promesses de la
philosophie, absoudre la providence du long règne du crime et
de la tyrannie.

[We want, in a word, to fulfill the course of nature, to
accomplish the destiny of mankind, to make good the promises
of philosophy, to absolve providence from the long reign of crime
and tyranny.]

Maximilien Robespierre, February 5, 1794

Acknowledgments

The subject of this work is the topic of the first course I designed, at Columbia University, in fall 1977. Over the past twenty-five years, I have taught much of this material in different forms, in undergraduate and graduate classes at Columbia, Purdue University, and the University of Virginia. I am grateful to all the students with whom I discussed the material in and out of class and to my colleagues at all three universities for countless enlightening discussions.

My former colleague, Dante Germino, read a previous draft of the entire manuscript and offered many valuable comments and suggestions. The material included in different chapters was either read by or discussed with numerous friends and colleagues, including Ernie Alleva, Colin Bird, Alan Cafruny, Daniel Devereux, Robert Fatton, Joshua Dienstag, Walter Odajnyk, Steven Wall, and Stephen White. My greatest debts are to the faculty and students of the Political Science Department at Loyola University of Chicago and other people who attended my Covey Lectures and raised interesting questions. I am especially indebted to Tom Engemann, Claudio Katz, and Rob Mayer. Rob especially was an excellent host during my week in Chicago and offered valuable advice, comments, and criticism of my chapter on Lenin. I also acknowledge my gratitude to the late Richard Hartigan, who was instrumental in establishing the lecture series.

Academic leave for the spring semester of 2000, provided by a University of Virginia Sesquicentennial grant, greatly aided preparation of first drafts of many chapters.

I thank my daughter, Caroline, for checking my French translations and, as ever, along with my wife, Margaret, and daughters, Susanna and Deborah, for moral support.

Introduction

The theme of this work is ideal societies and how to bring them into existence. Depictions of such societies are a recurrent motif in Western literature. Almost as long is a tradition of scholars reflecting on utopias and drawing conclusions from them. Valuable surveys have been presented by Frank Manuel and Fritzie Manuel, Krishan Kumar, and other scholars, while similarly valuable but more focused works include George Kateb's *Utopia and Its Enemies*.[1] To a certain extent my work will contribute to and, hopefully, advance this tradition. But there is a significant difference. In their magisterial survey, the Manuels describe the "functional division of labor" between writers who have developed utopias and activists who have attempted to realize them by establishing communes or launching revolutions with utopian aspirations. The Manuels' main interest is the former: "When we analyze popular millenarian or revolutionary movements, it is the content of the dreams, manifest or hidden, not the strategies for their realization, that primarily engages us."[2] My main concern is the latter. Unlike most students of utopia, I focus on strategies for realization and so also on impediments that must be overcome. In other words, I am more concerned with means than ends.

My subject is fundamental political — and moral — reform and how this can be brought about. I am less interested in actual attempts to change the world than in what has been written or thought about them and so less concerned with the practice of radical reform than its theory. But as we will see, important theorists of radical reform include practitioners, and some, such as Robespierre and Saint-Just and perhaps Lenin also, who are interesting as theorists largely because they were also practitioners. Theory and practice are not always separable, as in regard to Robespierre and Saint-Just or in other cases in which theories of radical reform must be read off from the actions of practitioners. For example, in his life of Lycurgus, Plutarch contrasts authors who used Lycurgus as a model and Lycurgus himself, who "was the author, not in writing but in reality, of a government which none else could so much as copy."[3] As we will see directly, Plutarch's *Lycurgus* has interesting things to say about radical reform, although it does so primarily in recounting the deeds of the legendary lawgiver. But for our purposes, the distinction between practice and theory is less important than that between reflections on means and on ends, although, of course, the nature of the latter will strongly affect the former.

As will be seen throughout this work, discussion of fundamental moral reform leads inexorably to questions of political power. Machiavelli classically articulated the claim that unarmed prophets go to the gallows. Recognizing something along these lines, the figures I discuss frequently concerned themselves with means of becoming armed. Thus the study of fundamental moral reform becomes deeply involved with themes of revolution, and subjects I address include the French and Russian Revolutions. But in spite of the rich variety of aspects of revolutions I could explore, I am concerned with the seizure of power only insofar as it is intended to be used in particular ways.

EDUCATIONAL REALISM

My central contentions in this work center on a specific connection between fundamental moral reform and political power. As we will see from a variety of perspectives, if people are to become fit for an ideal society, this must be as a result of concerted political action. Virtue will not arise spontaneously but must be inculcated. Thus to a large extent I argue from particular facts of human psychology or human nature. However, not in this work depends on far-reaching but vague claims about man's u mate potential or human nature in a grand sense. Rather, I am concerne with people as they are in existing societies, human beings that we our-selves both are and see around us. Marx might be right that there is no ultimate human nature, that in the final analysis what we are is an en-semble of social relations.[4] But even if we grant this, we cannot become substantially better unless social relations are changed in definite ways, through concerted human effort. In other words, if people are to be made virtuous, intensive education will be required, which in turn will require control of the educational environment and so of crucial aspects of society if not society as a whole.

It should be helpful to introduce a concept here. We can refer to recognition of the fact that virtue requires extensive education or condi-tioning as "educational realism" and so to a theorist who recognizes this as an "educational realist." Accordingly, central to our concerns are the political implications of educational realism, especially the need for suffi-cient political control to make the necessary education possible.

A great advantage of focusing on educational realism, as it seems to me, is its obvious truth. Setting aside larger questions of human na-ture, we can draw strong conclusions about human nature as it exists in modern societies and has existed throughout recorded history. Ob-servations along these lines have been used to criticize utopian aspira-tions, most notably of Karl Marx and related thinkers. But Sigmund Freud and Gaetano Mosca, to cite two notable examples, pursue what I view as a disadvantageous, three-stage strategy. From (a) observations con-cerning existing people, they derive (b) conclusions concerning ultimate human nature and then (c) criticize utopian theories on the basis of (b).[5]

The disadvantage of this strategy is seen in the obvious Marxian re-buttal that the full potential of human nature has not yet been seen. By focusing on educational realism, we can avoid intractable debates about man's ultimate nature. More clear cut are conclusions we can draw about the means needed to make existing people virtuous — though recognizing that both conceptions of virtue and necessary means will vary with differences in proposed ideal societies. Accordingly, I focus on this aspect of utopian theory and, again, its political implications.

.topia, I think it is useful to begin by reviewing mat-
The term "utopia" was of course coined by Thomas
ɔined the Greek *ou* for "no" and *topos* for "place." Clev-
in utopia puns on *eu,* the adverb "well"; and so utopia is
no place" but "good place." By tradition, standing opposed to
cal societies associated with "utopia" are departures from the ideal,
topias or "anti-utopias," presenting cautionary or critical alternative
visions, as frightening as utopias are enticing.

As generally understood, in terms of content utopias are limited to
accounts of societies that are substantially different from what exists. It
is difficult to draw the line between plans for political reform or revolution, especially ambitious plans, and utopia.[6] I will not attempt a precise
demarcation. But as I use the term here, a utopian society represents a
fundamental break with what exists, "a new state of being" or "the pattern for a human condition that is totally new by any standard."[7]

For our purposes, a central aspect of utopian thought is lack of concern with means of bringing postulated ideal societies into existence. We
can call a work that evinces little or no interest in realization a "pure
utopia," a term that can also be used to designate the society presented in
such a work. Many writers of what can be characterized as utopias wrote
to call attention to and condemn what they viewed as objectionable features of existing societies and so, conceivably, to bring about desired
reforms. But if a writer did no more than this, his creation should be
regarded as utopian.

Evidence of lack of concern with actually realizing proposed ideal
societies is seen in the literary form in which different writers present
their visions. Perhaps most familiar are descriptions of unexpected
encounters with unusual societies. Thus in *The City of the Sun,* Thomas
Campanella's protagonist, a Mariner, recounts how while on a voyage he
was forced to land on the island of Taprobane and what he saw there.
Something similar is seen in More's *Utopia,* which relates the unusual
discoveries of Raphael Hythloday — though, as we will see, his work is
actually a more complex case. The tradition of travelers' utopias goes
back to ancient times. For instance, Diodorus Siculus recounts the expe-

riences of a merchant, Iambulus, who through a complex chain of events came to observe the Islands of the Sun (II, 55–60).

A thematic variation on voyages to places unknown is Edward Bellamy's *Looking Backward,* in which the protagonist, Julian West, awakens from a deep sleep, begun in 1887, 113 years later, in the socialist utopia of the year 2000. There are other examples of ideal societies removed from existing society in time rather than space, projected into the future or the past.[8] Important contemporary examples are the constellation of unusual societies portrayed in works of science fiction. An ancient example is found in Plato's *Critias.* This work recounts the glories of ancient Athens—although, unfortunately, in a dialogue that is incomplete. The proper utopia in this work stands opposed to the ideal city of the *Republic,* which, removed in neither space nor time, is—I will argue—intended to be realized in this world.

At the opposite pole from utopianism on an imaginary continuum are theories that are intended to be realized. Among these, I include Jacobin theories. The actual Jacobins and their actions in the French Revolution are discussed below, in chapter 5. Throughout this work I use the term to designate a certain range of theories of moral reform, the essence of which has come to be associated with the revolutionary Jacobins. Briefly, as I use the term, a Jacobin theory includes an ideal vision that the author has not only thought about establishing, but has done so realistically, confronting the political obstacles to realization, including educational realism. Accordingly, at the heart of Jacobinism is state-controlled, moral education. The history of political theory contains a range of proposed means of reform. To some extent, my purpose in this work is to survey some of the more prominent possibilities. But because of what I take to be the truth of educational realism, I argue that Jacobinism is more plausible than other strategies. It is not just *a* theory of moral reform but arguably the one most likely to work in practice—although with a range of fundamental problems of its own, which I examine.

Questions of classification are complicated by the existence of alternatives to utopian theories other than Jacobinism. I examine several theorists who depart from pure utopianism in being seriously interested in realizing their ideals but do not fully confront the obstacles. In particular they propose to achieve their goals through persuasion alone. We can distinguish theorists who believe persuasion can be effective with the populace at large and others who believe in persuading possessors of political power. Among the former class, as we will see, we can locate the utopian socialists and Socrates. Notable examples of the latter class — who come close to Jacobins in important respects — are Thomas More and, as we will see, Plato, in particular episodes of both his life and his works. If the assumptions underlying educational realism are true, then persuasion-based theories cannot hope to succeed. As I discuss in chapter 2, Plato clearly came to this realization. The Jacobin-like political theory of the *Republic* can be seen to arise from the persuasion-based views of Socrates.

History has shown that the path to utopia is not easy. The past records few (if any) truly ideal societies, while actual attempts to realize the ideal have generally ended in terror and slaughter. We will look at possible strategies, their advantages and disadvantages, and, unfortunately, reasons why attempts to realize utopia are likely to fail.

Because of the breadth of the subject, I am not able to trace all attempts to realize utopia, or all analyses of such attempts, in theory and practice.[9] Rather I look at a series of exemplars and attempt to draw conclusions from them. These include ancient lawgivers, Lycurgus and Solon; Socrates and Plato; Machiavelli, More, and Rousseau; the French Revolution Jacobins, primarily Robespierre and Saint-Just; and the Marxian tradition. Some specific themes I discuss are as follows.

Because the means to radical reform entail confronting questions of power, discussion of Socrates and Plato is important, in that the former provides what I view as a classic instance of ignoring power. Plato, well aware of Socrates' oversight, sees the need for power but not a realistic way to it. In other words, Plato presents a clear account of the problem of radical reform and why it is so difficult to solve. According to Plato, power is necessary because the ideal society requires a basic change in human nature, which in turn requires intensive, state-controlled education. Thus Plato is an educational realist. The problems he addresses pose continuing challenges to would-be reformers who come after him. In spite of his general reputation as a pure utopian, Plato also provides a searching analysis of the path to political power. There are two main possibilities: reformers, in his case philosophers, can become rulers of cities, or rulers can become philosophers. While the latter alternative involves questions of seizing power, from which Plato withdraws, the former leaves the reformer depending on good fortune and factors beyond his control.

More's *Utopia* provides in-depth analysis of the latter of Plato's alternatives; Machiavelli's *Prince* and, especially, *Discourses* explore the former. In the *Discourses,* Machiavelli presents a classic account of conspiracies and a grim assessment of armed reformers. He also lays out a fundamental paradox at the heart of the politics of moral reform. It takes a bad man to ascend to power but a good man to use this in the interest of his state. And so where can this combination of attributes be found? With Rousseau, the ideas I have noted to this point advance significantly, in that Rousseau takes into account preconditions for radical reform. It is not merely a question of power; only certain kinds of societies can be reformed, and Rousseau lays out their parameters and adjusts his recommendations for specific societies accordingly.

Confronting head-on both the need for political power and Machiavelli's paradox, the Jacobin response is to rely on the reformer's virtue. As Plato was willing to entrust his philosopher-ruler with unaccountable power, the reformer in power can also be trusted, as long as he is the kind of person who does not have to be feared. Abundant difficulties are seen in two historical case studies, great modern revolutions with moral aspirations, the French and Russian. I examine the political theory of French Jacobins, especially Robespierre and Saint-Just, and Marxian ideas and their application to the situation in Russia by Lenin. In conjunction with Marx, I discuss the so-called utopian socialists, especially Charles Fourier, and Marx's anarchist opponent, Mikhail Bakunin.

The reader will be struck by the apparent incongruity of placing Plato's political theory in this context. At the present time, philosophers and many political theorists view Plato as a pure utopian, with no real interest in bringing his ideal society into existence. And so one of my main themes concerns a particular interpretation of Plato, of both the man and his works. Placing Plato's political theory in the tradition of attempts to realize the ideal society will show that Plato not only belongs in this tradition but also contributes to it. Not only were the concerns of Machiavelli, Robespierre, and Lenin his concerns, but his analyses of the politics of reform belong alongside those of his notorious successors. In a well-known remark, Alfred North Whitehead likens Western philosophy to a series of footnotes to Plato. To some extent, a central theme of my lectures is that in regard to the political theory of radical reform, Plato is also a pioneering figure. He lays out the problem and its main alternatives. With the philosophical ruthlessness that generally characterizes his political theory, he pursues the alternatives to their logical conclusion, while the unlikelihood of the ideal society can be read off from the difficulties he recounts.

To begin our exploration, I turn to what are perhaps the simplest accounts of putting theory into practice. I examine Lycurgus and Solon, familiar archetypes of the ancient lawgiver, especially as discussed by Plutarch in his *Lives*.

CHAPTER ONE

Ancient Lawgivers: Lycurgus and Solon

We begin our inquiry into realizing utopia by examining simple cases. For students of radical reform, the Greek city-states provide promising subject matter. Their small size and population make them far more plausible than modern nation-states, and Greek political theory abounds with proposals for reform. For our purposes, the most striking way in which reform was achieved was through the actions of a single individual, a lawgiver. Two classic instances were Lycurgus, in Sparta, and Solon, in Athens. I begin with these simple cases in order to draw attention to significant factors that should be considered in subsequent, more complex cases.

LYCURGUS

Perhaps the prime example of utopia made real in ancient history is the city of Sparta, especially as described in Plutarch's life of Lycurgus, the city's great lawgiver. In spite of problems assessing the accuracy of Plutarch's account, his presentation of Sparta's virtue and the institutions on which it rested exerted strong appeal to both theorists and reformers in subsequent centuries. Plutarch's depiction of Lycurgus is the locus classicus for the ideal lawgiver, able to create a republic of virtue mainly through sheer force of personality. There is no question about Sparta's political and military importance in the Greek world or its influence on Greek political theorists. Plato's ideal cities in the *Republic* and *Laws* are based heavily on Sparta, and the pull of Sparta affected Socrates as well. As Aristophanes writes in the *Birds:* "Sparta was all the rage. People grew their hair long, they starved themselves, they stopped having baths (like Socrates), they all carried walking sticks."[1]

In the tumultuous Greek world, in which virtually all cities were torn by revolution and civil war, an important attraction of Sparta was its relative stability. While other cities rose and fell, Sparta maintained an unchanging constitution and way of life for centuries. This is apparently the basis for Aristotle's inclusion of Sparta in the list of ideal cities discussed and criticized in Book II of the *Politics.* But more than this, there is something permanently stirring in the city's moral character, a combination of patriotism and military courage that has been emulated throughout history.

The role of Lycurgus in establishing Spartan institutions is shrouded in mystery. Plutarch makes no attempt to disguise the paucity of historical evidence or disagreement among authorities. He opens his *Life* as follows:[2] "Concerning Lycurgus the lawgiver, in general, nothing can be said that is not disputed" (*Lycurgus,* 1). This holds for different accounts of his birth, travels, and death, as well as his work as lawgiver and statesman. There is not even agreement about the time period in which he lived (*Lycurgus,* 1). While most modern scholars believe there was an actual historical figure, Lycurgus, who was responsible for important reforms in Sparta, there is no strong evidence to support this. Even if Lycurgus did live, modern scholars do little better than Plutarch in saying exactly when. The most reasonable estimate places his reforms early in the seventh century, but other scholars push these back into the ninth.[3] A. Andrewes gives a fair summation of the situation: "[I]f there was a real Lycurgus, we know nothing of him."[4]

The cloudiness of the historical record probably contributed to Lycurgus's mythical stature. Although it is not clear how much credit he deserves for the virtue of Sparta, he came to be identified with this, again perhaps most notably in the account of Plutarch.

Many features of Plutarch's Sparta are familiar and need not be reviewed here in detail. Most striking was an all-embracing social code, which insinuated itself into citizens' lives. The central feature was a system of intensive, state-run education, the *agōgē*. At the age of seven, children were removed from their families to be brought up communally. Older children were in charge of the younger. Throughout, the process was intended to foster qualities of discipline and toughness. Children lived under harsh conditions. They slept on beds made of reeds that they themselves tore, without knives, from the banks of the river Eurotas. From the age of twelve, they were given one cloak per year. Inadequately fed, they were forced to steal food to subsist, and those caught stealing were punished brutally. Plutarch reports that he himself saw several youths whipped to death for this offense (18). Legend extolled a young boy who having stolen a young fox, concealed it under his cloak when questioned. He allowed it to tear out his insides and died rather than have his theft detected (18). Throughout the entire education process, qualities of character were emphasized over abstract intelligence. Minimal reading and writing were taught, though youths learned music and verse, proper comportment, and to be terse and direct (laconic— from Laconia) in speech. Lycurgus did not regard children as "the peculiar property of their fathers, but rather as the common property of the *polis*" (15).

In a wider sense, education began before birth. Not any combination of man and woman was allowed to reproduce. As horses and dogs were carefully bred, so were Spartans. Especially promising parents were mated, while married men and women would seek out other partners for breeding purposes (15). At birth infants were inspected, with those found wanting exposed, at a place called Lesche (16). Spartan women were given a degree of freedom unusual in the Greek world. They exercised naked in public, and their vitality was deemed essential for the quality of their children. In this regard the Spartans were notably resistant to conventional opinions. What was deemed good for the state took precedence, as it did in the sanctioning of other unusual customs, notably the sharing of husbands and wives (15).

Throughout other areas of life the state took precedence over family. Marriage regulations forbade husbands and wives to live together until they were thirty. Husbands visited their wives by stealth, and it was said that many Spartans had children before they saw each others' faces in daylight (15).

Property was carefully regulated. Land was divided into equal parcels, owned by Spartan men. At some point in their lives, Spartan citizens were allotted parcels, which were farmed by helot-serfs, and they were not allowed to sell. As opposed to a prior situation of inequality and potential civil strife, possession of lots established equality in the state, and so Spartan citizens were "Equals" or "Peers." Although additional valuables were not confiscated, they had little effect on daily life. Throughout the state luxury was discouraged. Gold and silver were abolished, replaced with a cumbersome iron currency. Spartan dwellings were harshly austere, finished with no tool finer than an ax.

Spartans dined communally, at public messes (*sussitia*). Men ate in companies with, according to Plutarch, about fifteen members. Membership in a company had to be by unanimous consent; the objection of one member would keep a candidate out (12). It is likely that members of a *sussition* were also a military company. One fought alongside one's messmates, no doubt contributing to battlefield courage and cohesiveness.

To make sure the young were properly educated, Lycurgus used the entire state as a school for virtue. The young were to be exposed constantly to examples of Spartan virtue, and nothing else. Toward this end they were forbidden to travel abroad, and non-Spartans were barred from the city, lest they bring with them strange doctrines and customs that could corrupt the young (27).

As a result of Lycurgus's arrangements, the Spartans became the fiercest soldiers in Greece. Without economic or family concerns to occupy them, they turned their attention to war. So intensive was their training that they viewed the rigors of battle as a relief. Plutarch clearly delights in recounting the Spartans' methodical entry into combat:

> And when at last they were drawn up in battle array and the enemy was at hand, the king sacrificed the customary she-goat, commanded all the warriors to set garlands upon their heads, and ordered the

pipers to pipe the strains of the hymn to Castor; then he himself led
off in a marching paean, and it was a sight equally grand and terrify-
ing when they marched in step with the rhythm of the flute, without
any gap in their line of battle, and with no confusion in their souls,
but calmly and cheerfully moving with the strains of their hymn into
the deadly fight. (22)

Having defeated their enemies, they refrained from slaughtering them,
which also encouraged surrender.

Tales of the courage of Spartan soldiers survive and still have power
to stir. Notable is the engagement at Thermopylae during the Persian wars,
when three hundred Spartans willingly sacrificed themselves. Herodotus
recounts how during the battle three times Xerxes leapt from his throne,
fearing for his huge army. Finally, with their weapons shattered, the Spartans "resisted to the last, with their swords, if they had them, and, if not,
with their hands and teeth," until they were overwhelmed.[5] Herodotus
says that he made himself acquainted with the names of all three hundred Spartans, "because they deserve to be remembered" (7.224). Their
courage was honored with a monument inscribed with the most famous
of military epitaphs: "Stranger, tell the Spartans that we obeyed their laws
and are buried here" (Herodotus, 7.228; my trans.).

Many other details of Spartan courage and virtue could be recounted. Other admirable aspects of the polity could also be discussed,
including, notably, the balanced or "mixed" constitution, which im-
pressed later political theorists.[6] But what I have mentioned should
suffice to convey the distinctive qualities of the Spartan polity. Their
system was not without severe flaws. Most important was the treatment
of enslaved helots. As they greatly outnumbered the Spartans, they were
suppressed ruthlessly. Toward that end, Spartan youth learned to kill
helots by stealth. To legitimize this practice, the Spartans declared war
on the helots each year (28). Thucydides reports an episode during the
Peloponnesian War. Fearing a helot revolt, the Spartans encouraged the
most ambitious helots to volunteer for military service, implying that
they would be freed. Some two thousand volunteered. They were garlanded and marched around the temple but then disappeared, eliminated by the Spartans (Thucydides, 4.80). Although Plutarch records

such occurrences, he gives them little attention, and he refuses to believe
that Lycurgus was responsible for them (28).

Having seen something of Sparta's legendary virtue, I turn to our
main question, how Lycurgus's system was established. The short answer
here is that because of gaps in the evidence, we do not know. Even if
Lycurgus existed, we cannot be sure how he managed to implement his
system. The fullest account is Plutarch's, which I will supplement with
brief remarks from Herodotus.

According to Plutarch, Lycurgus was from the Spartan royal family
and had attained power as the regent or guardian for the infant king,
Charilaus. The selfless way Lycurgus handled this position gave him a
reputation for virtue (Plutarch, *Lycurgus, 3*). When he eventually saw the
opportunity to bring about reforms, he rejected modest change. According to Plutarch:

> He was convinced that a partial change of the laws would be of no
> avail whatsoever, but that he must proceed as a physician would with
> a patient who was debilitated and full of all sorts of diseases; he must
> reduce and alter the existing temperament by means of drugs and
> purges, and introduce a new and different regimen. (5)[7]

Accordingly, Lycurgus's reform of Sparta was fundamental, a radical
reordering of not only the political system but the city's entire way of life.
With this end in mind, Lycurgus began to recruit allies. He worked to win
the chief men of Sparta to his cause, gradually building up a following.
"And when the time for action came, he ordered thirty of the chief men
to go armed into the market-place at break of day, to strike consternation
and terror into those of the opposite party" (5). The King at first took
flight but soon was convinced to return and support the enterprise. With
his position firmly established, Lycurgus undertook his reforms.

It is interesting to note that when he encountered resistance, Lycurgus
did not respond with force. According to Plutarch's account, the rich re-
sented the institution of common tables. Banding together, they denounced
Lycurgus and threw stones at him. As Lycurgus fled, a youth struck him
with a stick, putting out his eye. Lycurgus shamed his countrymen with
the sight of his face. They turned over the assailant to him. But Lycurgus

did not punish the youth. Through exposure to his virtuous character, he won the youth over as a supporter (*Lycurgus*, 11).

According to legend, after all his reforms were enacted and he was pleased with the overall system, Lycurgus called an assembly and got the Spartans to agree to observe the laws and leave them unchanged until he returned from consulting the oracle at Delphi. He then left the state, never to return, binding the Spartans to perpetual observance of his laws (29).

As recounted by Herodotus, the tale is simpler. According to the historian, "after [Lycurgus] became guardian of his nephew Leobotas, king of Sparta, and acted as his regent; . . . as soon as he received this appointment he made fundamental changes in the laws, and took good care that the new ones should not be broken" (Herodotus, 1.65).

Neither Plutarch nor Herodotus provides much information on the conditions that made Lycurgus's radical reforms necessary. We have noted that Plutarch's Lycurgus viewed his state as radically defective and so beyond help by partial remedies. But the details of these ills are not explained, aside from an account of "dreadful" economic inequality, which bred "insolence and envy and crime and luxury" (*Lycurgus*, 8). Herodotus notes, simply, that before Lycurgus's reforms the Spartans had been "the worst governed people in Greece" (1.65). Aside from the fact that Plutarch's report is more elaborate, his account and Herodotus's are basically similar, with important exceptions. Given our overall lack of information about Lycurgus, it is not possible to decide which account is more accurate. But aside from the conflict over the identity of the Spartan king, the details are not irreconcilable. The main difference is that Plutarch's Lycurgus was able to rely on more than the force of his personality. He had an armed contingent, able to intimidate potential foes. It says something about the size of Greek cities that a force of thirty men was apparently sufficient. This also tells us something about the relative social harmony in Sparta, as does the fact that subsequent violence amounted to little more than street fighting. If Herodotus's account is correct, even the minimal coercion described by Plutarch was not necessary. However, given the all-embracing character of Lycurgus's reforms, it is likely that Plutarch's account is more accurate, that more than the force of character or persuasion alone was required.

Most important in regard to Lycurgus as reformer is the extent of his changes. He reconfigured the social and educational systems as well as the constitution or political system. Clearly, reformed social and educational aspects of the state supported the constitution, as for centuries Sparta was known for its political stability. It is important to recognize that Lycurgus's system was not self-sustaining. It depended on intensive education. As we have seen, from early childhood—perhaps from before birth—Spartans were carefully molded to fit their society, while infants who were unlikely to fit in were cast aside. Thus, in addition to a radically new society, Lycurgus mandated that the resources of the state be harnessed to instill the necessary virtues in the citizenry. As I discuss in subsequent chapters, education, notably intensive, state-controlled education, is a central theme in the political theory of radical reform. Even though Lycurgus's Sparta was an all-embracing, enclosed social system, Lycurgus did not believe that growing up in such an atmosphere was enough; intensive training was also necessary.

As noted in the introduction, we can refer to a theorist's recognition of the need for intensive education to mold citizens as "educational realism." We should recognize two elements here: (a) a claim that people are to some extent malleable, so that education has the potential to work in significant ways; and (b) a claim that intensive, directed education is necessary to inculcate the desired characteristics. In other words, citizens are not born with the relevant characteristics, nor do they arise spontaneously; they must be inculcated.

In Lycurgus, then, we see three main themes in the political theory of radical reform: (i) a radical program, extending beyond constitutional or political reform; (ii) given the extent of the reforms, resort to some measure of coercion to bring them about; and (iii) educational realism, in regard to shaping the citizens to the requirements of the new society. But in spite of these elements, Lycurgus's reforms fell short in two ways. First, not unexpectedly, the resulting social system was not entirely ideal. In Book I of the *Laws*, Plato criticizes Sparta for its overly narrow conception of virtue, based on military courage (626c–31b). Proof of the inadequacy of this conception of virtue is the rapid decline of Spartan morals once the Peloponnesian War was won. In Book IV of the *Politics*, Aristotle distinguishes between different kinds of ideal states. Among kinds he lists are the most ideal, "if no external circumstance stands in the way," as opposed to "that which is best under assumed conditions" (*Pol.* 1288b22–27).[8] The Spartan polity was clearly the latter. The need to control the captive helot population was a primary consideration in shaping the entire state. This undoubtedly was one reason for Sparta's extreme emphasis on military virtue, and, as we have seen, ruthless means were used. Presumably, without the pressure of these external circumstances, the Spartans could have pursued a more rounded conception of virtue. But then again, one can ask if other moral ideals would have enabled the state to succeed to the same degree.

The second difficulty concerns the first generation. If we assume that Plutarch's account is correct, then it is conceivable that once Lycurgus's system was up and running it became successful and self-sustaining. The combined educational and all-inclusive social systems would have molded the Spartans, making them supportive of the system, willing, as we have seen, cheerfully to lay down their lives in its defense. But the question still remains how the generation of Spartans with whom Lycurgus had to deal were persuaded to change their ways so completely. They had not been brought up under the requisite conditions, nor had they experienced the rigors of the *agōgē*. In Plutarch's account Lycurgus was able to use a measure of coercion to exact compliance, and I have noted the story of how he tricked the Spartans into promising perpetual compliance with his laws. But still, the process of moving from a nonvirtuous, presumably corrupt existing condition to a virtuous state of affairs is not adequately explained. Under educational realism it is assumed that people are to some extent malleable and so capable of being shaped by their environment. But if a good environment can make people virtuous, a bad environment should have the opposite effect. In Plutarch's account we find no adequate explanation of how the corrupted first generation was prevented from corrupting their young, thereby throwing the state off course from the outset.

SOLON

Distinctive features of Lycurgus's reforms can be highlighted by comparing them to the work of another prototypical ancient lawgiver, Solon, again primarily as described by Plutarch. In an immediate sense discussing Solon is easier than Lycurgus, for two reasons. First, Solon was surely a historical personage. Although legends have sprung up about him as well, there is much stronger evidence. Second and of great interest for us, what Solon set out to achieve was far more limited than Lycurgus's total reform.

The early sixth century was a time of civil strife in Athens. Athenian law allowed borrowers to pledge future produce of their farms or even their own persons as security for loans. This resulted in many people being effectively or actually enslaved. According to Plutarch, the disparity between the poor and the rich had left the city "in an altogether perilous condition," and it seemed to many that a tyranny was the only way to overcome the difficulties (*Solon*, 13). Under these circumstances, people turned to Solon, making him archon and mediator of the crisis (*Solon*, 14; Aristotle, *Const. Ath.* 5). Solon was acceptable to the poor because he was honest and to the rich because he was well-off.

Although both sides had great hopes, Solon essentially sided with the poor. He mandated forgiving all debts and forbade pledges of persons or future produce for loans (*Solon*, 15). These actions pleased no one. The rich were angry about losing their money; the poor had hoped for more, redivision of the land (16). Empowered as lawgiver, Solon enacted sweeping reforms. He instituted a new criminal code, far less stringent than the existing code, which had been drawn up by Draco. He enacted significant constitutional reforms, dividing the Athenians into classes, according to wealth, which were assigned different governmental privileges. He instituted a council of four hundred to oversee the Assembly, and perhaps most significant in the long run, he opened up the Assembly and jury service to the poor, probably unwittingly helping to lay the groundwork for extreme democracy in Athens (*Solon*, 18). Other reforms encouraged Athens's movement from an agricultural to a commercial economy, including encouraging foreigners to emigrate to Athens to work as merchants or craftsmen.[9]

Thus we can see that in scope Solon's reforms were substantially different from those of Lycurgus. Though of great moment and significance for the subsequent history of Athens, they did not represent a complete break with the past. Whereas Lycurgus's reforms went beyond the political to complete overhaul of social and educational aspects of the state, Solon's essentially remained political. There were exceptions, notably canceling debts and outlawing loans based on personal security, but for the most part Solon reformed the laws and constitution and altered the legal rights of citizens.

Solon was aware of the limited character of his reforms. When asked if he had made the best laws for Athens, he responded: "The best they would receive" (*Solon,* 15). On the whole his activities were characterized by moderation, although his reforms pleased neither rich nor poor and did not lead to an end of instability in the state. At one point he had the opportunity to take power in Athens, as despot. This alternative was widely supported by people who believed that the stranglehold of the rich could be broken only by despotic power.[10] But Solon did not choose this path, to spare Athens "tyranny and violence," and believed this would be one of his claims to future fame (14). Had Solon been more ambitious or ruthless, he might have taken power. It is possible that the main reason he did not was his moderate character. On the other hand, had he not been recognized as having such a character, he probably would not have been elevated to a position of authority in the first place.

Plutarch notes that in comparison to those of Lycurgus, Solon's reforms were slight, as he did not redistribute the land or make all men equal. Plutarch writes:

> But Lycurgus was eleventh in descent from Heracles, and had been king in Lacedaemon for many years. He therefore had great authority, many friends, and power to support his reforms in the commonwealth. He also employed force rather than persuasion, insomuch that he actually lost his eye thereby, and most effectually guaranteed the safety and unanimity of the city by making all its citizens neither poor nor rich. (*Solon,* 16)

Solon, in contrast, "was a man of the people and modest station; yet he in no wise acted short of his real power, relying as he did only on the wishes of the citizens and their confidence in him" (*Solon,* 16). There is a clear correlation here, or perhaps a rule of political reform. One can go only as far as his means will take him. Solon had access to more drastic means but shied away from them. Whether going down that road would have improved the situation of his city is impossible to say. But not having resort to force, Solon confined his attention to the laws and constitution. Though he made impressive alterations in these areas, because he refrained from overturning the social and educational systems, he should not be considered a radical reformer.

CHAPTER TWO

Socratic Reform

My brief examination of Solon and Lycurgus indicates the importance of political power in attempts radically to reform existing societies. I pursue this theme in this chapter, from a rather different perspective, by examining central themes in Plato's political theory. I argue that the need to couple reform and political power is a central theme in Plato and that it is developed in the early and middle dialogues through Plato's critique of the idea that reform can be accomplished through persuasion alone, which is an idea he associated with Socrates. Plato's own position, then, as classically argued in the *Republic,* grows out of his rejection of this other possibility. These are controversial and currently unfashionable assertions about how Plato's political theory should be read, though claims concerning Plato's abiding interest in questions of reform were common in the scholarly community until fairly recently. Not only do I believe that such a heavily politicized reading of Plato's political theory is accurate, but I argue that much of what Plato says on these issues is persuasive. Though often dismissed as hopelessly utopian — or, alternatively, as a steadfast and nonpolitical opponent of utopian political theory — Plato's views on questions of reform are better grounded than those of many theorists who are taken far more seriously on these issues.

INTERPRETATION OF THE EARLY DIALOGUES

To establish my interpretation of Plato's political theory, I am forced to address highly difficult and controversial issues at the heart of Plato scholarship. Thus something brief must be said about the Socratic problem, the order of Plato's dialogues, and how the dialogues should be read. For obvious reasons, I do not want to get bogged down in these issues. They are so controversial that general agreement among scholars is probably impossible. But I should note that on each of these contentious issues my position is both commonsensical and widely held. If we collect the relevant evidence and assess it according to the usual historical procedures, it strongly suggests the account of Plato's political theory that I develop.

I discuss six main topics. First are the three issues in Plato scholarship noted above.[1] I then move on to the fourth theme, the political theory of Plato's Socrates, as presented in the early dialogues. As we will see, strong evidence for this account of Socrates is found in Plato's critique of this position. Thus I trace this line of criticism through several early dialogues, most notably the *Gorgias,* and work out its development into the political theory of the *Republic.* The fifth topic is Plato's political theory in the *Republic,* which is supported by analysis of historical evidence and brief discussion of the later political dialogues, especially the *Seventh Epistle* and *Laws.* Sixth and last, I defend this interpretation of Plato's political theory by examining an important contemporary alternative reading, that associated with Leo Strauss and Allan Bloom, which will be found wanting on both methodological and substantive grounds. The first four themes are discussed in this chapter, the fifth and sixth in the next.

Although there are considerable difficulties in dealing with questions of overall interpretation of Plato's dialogues, they must be addressed as preliminaries to any discussion of the corpus or parts of it. Whether consciously or not, the interpreter must make assumptions concerning these issues; it is not possible to have no positions, as it is impossible to answer questions without any methodology. Because of the nature of the evidence, no position is entirely without difficulties. My aim is to present the overall account that makes the most sense of the evidence, with the fewest difficulties.

By employing different sources of evidence, both external and internal, it is possible to divide the dialogues into groups that can be placed at different stages of Plato's career. The dialogues contain few references to historical or political events that allow us to date the composition of individual dialogues.[2] However, careful analysis of elements of Plato's use of language and literary style allows the dialogues to be compared to the *Laws*, which, on good authority, is the last dialogue to have been written.[3] Different sorts of stylometric analysis have been worked out by scholars and have yielded general agreement on the existence of a group of late dialogues, written in relatively close proximity to the *Laws*. This includes the *Theaetetus, Sophist, Statesman, Philebus,* and *Timaeus*. There is less agreement on the other dialogues. But on the whole the evidence supports division between two groups, which are generally referred to as Plato's early and middle dialogues, although the evidence does not allow us to identify the order of composition within groups or to draw precise boundary lines between them. But with some assurance works such as the *Apology, Crito, Ion, Hippias Minor, Laches, Charmides,* and *Protagoras* can be identified as early works, while the great cycle of middle dialogues includes the *Meno, Phaedo, Symposium, Republic,* and *Phaedrus*. There is less certainty about other works, for example, the *Euthydemus* and *Cratylus,* or whether the *Parmenides* should be identified as a middle or late work. For obvious reasons, I do not wish to explore these issues here and will not make claims that depend on specific dating of these works.

It would distract us from more important concerns to discuss results of stylometric analysis in more detail. But it is important to note that conclusions drawn through these means are supported by analysis of the dramatic and philosophical aspects of the dialogues. To begin with the former, the early dialogues tend to be highly dramatic. In the *Apology* Plato's Socrates presents an unusual account of his philosophical activity. Claiming to lack moral knowledge, Socrates does not teach a doctrine but examines claims to knowledge made by other people, through the notorious Socratic *elenchos*. The *elenchos* is an important subject of this chapter, and I will return to it in detail. What is important to note here is that many of the dialogues depict Socrates' practice of the *elenchos,* especially in regard to moral subjects. In the *Laches* he examines prominent interlocutors on the nature of courage; in the *Charmides* he does something similar in regard to temperance. The *Euthyphro* concerns examination of the vain and pompous title character in regard to the nature of piety, much as Book I of the *Republic* depicts examination of a series of interlocutors in regard to the nature of justice. These works, and others one can name, end inconclusively; instead of establishing a definite philosophical doctrine, they result in general confessions of ignorance on the subject under discussion. It should be noted, however, that although little firm philosophical theory is established in these works, their presentation of Socratic philosophical activity also includes a series of philosophical views Socrates is depicted as holding in other sources of evidence. These views can be reconstructed and help to flesh out the more straightforward account of central Socratic principles presented in the *Apology*.

The middle dialogues are notably less dramatic. Instead of unsuccessful inquiry into their subject matter, they consist largely of exposition by a Socrates who provides answers to fundamental questions of human existence. In these works the question-and-answer format is largely an excrescence. So immaterial does the role of Socrates' interlocutors become that F. M. Cornford, one of the great classics scholars of the twentieth century, simply edits their responses out of his edition of the *Republic*.[4]

Along with the change in the dramatic nature of the dialogues comes evolution of their doctrine. Roughly and briefly, the middle dialogues contain an entire, developed theory — Platonism — centering on the theory of Forms and the immortality of the soul, that is absent from the earlier works. Though there are occasional hints of the Forms in certain early works, notably the *Lysis* and *Euthyphro,* on the whole this doctrine is absent from the earlier works. Whereas the *Meno, Gorgias, Phaedo, Republic,* and *Phaedrus* recount variations on the theme of transmigration of souls, Socrates in the *Apology* is notably agnostic, and among the ideas of the afterlife that he entertains, none involves transmigration.

To make sense of these differences between the early and middle dialogues, it is natural to assume that one of Plato's central aims in the early dialogues was to present the distinctive character and teaching of Socrates. Because Socrates did not expound a doctrine, his teaching could be conveyed best through depiction of his elenctic activity. When Plato's aim changed to expounding the philosophical theory that we associate with his name, his interest in depicting Socrates became less important.

Although he retained the dialogue form, this became largely a shell, the contents of which centered increasingly on Socratic lectures on Platonic doctrine. Confirmation of this course of development is that in the late dialogues, when Plato's interest in representing Socrates had faded still further, Socrates largely disappears from the compositions. The doctrine Plato wished to propound is put into the mouths of other characters — Timaeus in the *Timaeus,* the Eleatic Stranger in the *Sophist* and the *Statesman,* and the Athenian Stranger in the *Laws.* In the last of these, Socrates is entirely absent. Presumably, Socrates is retained in the *Theaetetus* and *Philebus,* in spite of the doctrinal movement from the early dialogues, because the subject matter of these compositions (the nature of knowledge in the former and the value of pleasure in the latter) is closer to that of the early dialogues than in the other late works.

This account of the development of Plato's corpus leaves open a fundamental question concerning the early dialogues. I have noted that one of Plato's chief aims is representing the character and teaching of Socrates. But this view is compatible with different accounts of the extent to which the views presented in the early works are those of the historical Socrates, as Plato recalled him, or are Plato's own — whether those he held throughout his career or only when he was working on the early dialogues. The so-called Socratic problem cannot be discussed in detail here, but I believe that appeal to evidence outside the dialogues strongly suggests a particular line of interpretation. The evidence indicates that the early dialogues are largely concerned with depicting the historical Socrates, as Plato understood him, and that as he moved into the more dogmatic, less dramatic middle dialogues the content of the dialogues became increasingly Plato's own. Thus we can contrast the Socratic early dialogues and the Platonic middle and late (though there are changes between these two groups). For ease of reference, we can refer to the views presented in the early works as those of "Socrates" and of the middle and late as those of "Plato"—but without losing sight of the fact that in the middle and some of the late works, the views in question are put into the mouth of Socrates. This "Socrates," though, should be kept distinct from the historical Socrates and viewed as largely a mouthpiece for Platonic philosophy.

A variety of concerns support this interpretation. First, the "Socratic dialogue" (*Sokratikos logos*) was an established literary genre (Aristotle,

Poetics 1447b9). Plato was not the only practitioner. Although most examples of the genre are lost, in addition to the works of Plato, we have numerous dialogues by Xenophon and fragments from Aeschines. The genre is said to have originated as followers and associates of Socrates began to write down his actual conversations, to preserve his unique teaching. According to Diogenes Laertius, the first practitioner was a cobbler named Simon (D. L., II, 122–23). Something along these lines is depicted in the "frame conversation" of the *Theaetetus*. In this context Eucleides of Megara, one of Socrates' actual pupils, repeats a conversation between Socrates and the title character that he says he wrote down (*Tht.* 142c–43a). However, even if Socrates' followers set out to recount his actual teaching, it is likely that they interpreted this quite differently. There were a number of "minor Socratic schools" in antiquity, each of which traced its teaching back to Socrates, although these differed remarkably. The school of Antisthenes taught Cynic-like physical hardihood and that virtue is sufficient for happiness, while Aristippus, founder of the Cyrenaics, argued for a good life based on physical pleasure. The compositions of Plato and Xenophon differ substantially. Not only are Plato's middle and late dialogues not faithful to the historical Socrates, but the same is true of several of Xenophon's compositions, which scholars universally interpret as presentations of Xenophon's own views put into the mouth of Socrates.[5] However, a number of Xenophon's works are likely to be much closer to the historical Socrates. There is considerable overlap between these, especially the *Memorabilia,* and Plato's early dialogues, which had similar intentions. It is likely that much Socratic teaching is found in the areas of agreement between these groups of works, although because Plato's account is immeasurably richer and deeper, it is more likely accurately to reflect the actual phenomenon of Socrates.

The extant evidence suggests that a series of themes were regularly addressed in the Socratic literature. Both Plato and Xenophon wrote apologies, or accounts of Socrates' defense before the jury, and symposia. Extant among works of Aeschines are fragments of a dialogue between Socrates and Alcibiades, thus addressing a theme present in Plato's corpus in several works, most notably the *Alcibiades I* (if it is genuine, on which more below) and *Symposium.*[6] However, things are complicated by the fact that compositions on similar tropes are remarkably different. The implications for interpreting Plato's *Apology* are discussed below.

The claim that Plato's early dialogues are concerned with presenting the teaching of the historical Socrates (as Plato understood him) is supported by the best extant historical evidence concerning Socrates' philosophical views—that of Aristotle. The crucial point here is that Aristotle clearly distinguishes the philosophical views of Socrates and Plato, attributing the doctrine of Forms to the latter but not the former, in a way that corresponds to the philosophical differences between the early and middle dialogues (Aristotle, *Metaphysics* 987a, 1078b). The contrast in this area is well known and, once again, provides strong evidence that Plato's middle dialogues present his own philosophical views as opposed to those of Socrates, although it appears that Plato has done more than simply to present his own ideas. Rather, according to the most reasonable account, through the sequence of dialogues, Plato guides the reader through a series of stages that may well correspond to the intellectual process that led him from Socrates' attempts to wrestle with important problems to his own fully developed answers.[7] For our purposes it is necessary to recognize that the same sort of contrast between Socratic and Platonic views in the area of metaphysics can be drawn in moral psychology. In several contexts Aristotle dismissively criticizes Socrates' views, which he contrasts with those of Plato, in a way that corresponds to doctrinal differences in the early and middle dialogues. The contrasts here are discussed below. It is also important to realize that in the area of moral psychology, Plato's position can be seen to be founded on criticism and rejection of the Socratic view. We are also able to distinguish Socrates' and Plato's views on the means of bringing about fundamental moral reform, which are bound up with the two thinkers' respective psychological views. Once again Plato's view can be seen to grow out of criticism and rejection of that of Socrates.

The precise extent to which the philosophical views advanced in the early dialogues are those of Socrates alone, free from an admixture of content supplied from Plato, cannot be determined. Once again the considerations we have reviewed constitute a strong case that their content is largely

Socratic, although presentation of Socrates in these works is carefully manipulated by Plato to facilitate the development of his own philosophical and political views.

SOCRATES' MISSION

The political theory of the early dialogues—which I refer to as the theory of Socrates—is bound up with the unique mission of moral reform that Socrates recounts in the *Apology* and in the practice of which he is depicted in many dialogues.[8] At first sight this might seem an unusual claim. The Socrates of Plato's dialogues seems a poor candidate for the list of proponents of wholesale moral reform. Socrates explicitly distances himself from his city's political system and passes his time arguing with people—with everyone and anyone—about often arcane matters of moral philosophy. But in keeping with the contrast between appearance and underlying reality that is central to Socrates' notorious irony, extremely serious concerns underlay Socrates' activity. To understand this, we must examine the unique method through which Socrates practiced philosophy, the *elenchos*. As we will see, more than a philosophical technique, in the hands of Socrates, the *elenchos* was intended to be a method of moral reform. An additional reason why Socrates' activity of reform is not adequately recognized is because it depended on a series of unusual philosophical views to which he subscribed, which we must also explore.

Elenchos is the Greek word for "test" or "refutation." As practiced by Socrates, it was a means of examining people's moral beliefs, which was bound up with examination of the way they lived their lives. To see what the *elenchos* entails, we can examine an instance of its working, which we can extrapolate from the *Laches*. In this work the blunt, anti-intellectual title character, an Athenian general, asked to define courage, says that "anyone who is willing to stay at his post and face the enemy and does not run away" is courageous (*Lach.* 190e). Greek warfare during the fifth and fourth centuries centered on clashes between lines of heavily armed foot soldiers, hoplites. When the line of one side broke, this generally signaled defeat and placed its hoplites in danger of their lives. Thus Laches' answer touches on something central to courage—military courage—and so contains an element of truth. But the definition is obviously too rigid and too narrow, and Socrates has little trouble finding a counterexample. At the great battle of Plataea, in 479, the Spartans performed a complicated maneuver. The best trained and disciplined army at that time, the Spartans were alone in being able to reconstitute their line after it was broken. Accordingly, in the face of the Persians, they feigned disorganization and retreated. The Persians, seeing the Spartan line broken, charged in for the kill—disorganizing their own ranks. At this point the Spartans re-formed and annihilated the Persians.

Faced with this example, Laches is forced to recognize that there is more to courage than staying in one's place in the battle line. And so he proposes a more abstract and provocative definition—that courage is a certain endurance of the soul. Socrates focuses on this, with similar results, and the process continues until all parties to the conversation, including Socrates, admit that they do not know what courage is, and the dialogue comes to an end.

Looking at an encounter like this, the reader naturally wonders what has been accomplished. This can be seen if we lay out the structure of an *elenchos* somewhat schematically.

A. The interlocutor presents a view on some moral question. We can call this view 1.
B. Socrates shows that view 1 is inadequate in some important respect.
C. The interlocutor, recognizing the problems with 1, brings forth another opinion; call this view 2.

What is interesting here is that in content views 1 and 2 are likely to be similar, although 2 will likely be more sophisticated and so a better answer to the question. But what interests Socrates is a different respect in which it is superior. As the *elenchos* continues and 2 is refuted, the interlocutor is led to propose other opinions, views 3 and 4, and so on. What most interests Socrates is that along with view 2, these other opinions are products of conscious reflection. Whereas 1 is probably an opinion the interlocutor had been taught or heard somewhere, or otherwise soaked in from the environment, subsequent opinions result from his reflection on the problem at hand and his attempts to answer it. In other words, as a result of the *elenchos,* the subject is led to think about moral questions for himself.

Socrates places great emphasis on the difference between moral opinions that are simply absorbed from one's environment and those that are products of conscious reflection. He believes that the latter but not the former are worthy of a human being, that it is a lower form of human existence to act on the basis of principles one has not adopted oneself. As Socrates says in the *Apology,* "the unexamined life is not worth living." To think and talk about virtue "is the greatest good to man" (*Ap.* 38a). Socrates' defense of his life in the *Apology* is bound up with the mission he has assumed to perform elenctic examination on all his fellow citizens. He describes himself as a gadfly, attached to Athens as to a horse, "which, though large and well bred, is sluggish on account of his size and needs to be aroused by stinging" (*Ap.* 30e). For Socrates, thinking about moral questions for oneself is a central part of what it means to "care for one's soul."

There is more to Socrates' moral philosophy and more to caring for the soul than thinking about moral issues for oneself. Socrates teaches the priority of certain values over others, that it is shameful to be concerned more for wealth and honor than for "wisdom and truth and the perfection of [one's] soul" (*Ap.* 29d–e). But in addition, one must be just; it is never permissible to do wrong. The connections here are not clearly worked out in Plato's early dialogues or in other evidence we possess about Socrates. But clearly, Socrates preaches that pursuing justice and refraining from injustice is central to caring for one's soul. In the *Crito* Socrates describes the soul as that within us "which is injured by the wrong (*adikon*) and improved by the right (*dikaion*)" and argues that with a tainted soul life is not worth living (*Crito* 47e). He argues that no harm can come to a good man and so that virtue is sufficient for happiness (*Ap.* 41c–d).[9]

The implications of this position are drawn in the *Gorgias,* in which Socrates presents the great paradox that it is better to suffer wrong than to commit it, with the consequences of suffering wrong described in excruciating detail (*Grg.* 473b–c). There is no serious attempt in the early dialogues to demonstrate the connections between justice or virtue and happiness. A full-scale demonstration of this position must wait until the

Republic. It is possible that Socrates' views concerning the sufficiency of virtue for happiness rest on a kind of religious faith. But whatever we think on this question, it is clear that Plato regards this as a revolutionary moral teaching. As Callicles says in the *Gorgias,* if what Socrates says is true, "won't human life have to be turned completely upside down?" (*Grg.* 481c).

One reason Socrates places great store in the content of people's ethical views is his belief that these decisively affect human conduct. To appreciate his mission of moral reform, one must recognize the distinctive psychological views that constitute its philosophical underpinning. Because of their great importance for his political activity—if not exactly his political theory—we must examine Socrates' psychological views in some detail.

Socrates' distinctive ethical views are bound up with a series of moral claims known as the Socratic paradoxes. The two main ones are that "virtue is knowledge" and that "all wrongdoing is caused by ignorance"— otherwise expressed as "all wrongdoing is involuntary" or "nobody does wrong willingly." That virtue is knowledge is familiar Socratic doctrine, touched on in many contexts in the dialogues. This is at the heart of Socrates' familiar analogy between virtue and knowledge of different crafts. According to Alcibiades in the *Symposium,* Socrates is always talking about "pack asses, smiths, cobblers, and tanners" (*Symp.* 221e). As knowledge of shoemaking makes one a shoemaker, so knowledge of virtue makes one virtuous. Socrates employs an argument precisely along these lines against Gorgias in the *Gorgias* (460b–c). Closely parallel arguments attributed to Socrates by Xenophon and Aristotle leave little doubt that this was an argument actually employed by Socrates (Xenonophon, *Mem.* 4.2.20; Aristotle, *EE* 1216b6–9). Although we do not find a clear account of the relevant knowledge in the early dialogues, it is apparently knowledge of good and evil. In both the *Laches* and the *Charmides,* Socrates suggests the central role this kind of knowledge plays in virtue. In keeping with the Socratic belief in the unity of the virtues, it appears that courage and the other virtues are aspects of the knowledge of good and evil.[10]

Exactly how possession of this knowledge makes one virtuous is not explained in the early dialogues and so is difficult to make out. But according to the most likely reconstruction, Socrates subscribes to a form of psychological egoism. He believes that people will follow their beliefs as to what is best for them. As he argues in the *Protagoras*, "knowledge is something noble and able to govern man"; "whoever learns what is good and what is bad will never be swayed by anything to act otherwise than as knowledge bids" (*Prt.* 352c). Couple this with conviction that it is always in a person's interest to be virtuous, and the conclusion follows that if people are aware of this, they will always be virtuous.[11] Support for this extremely intellectualistic account of Socrates' conception of virtue is provided by Aristotle, in the *Magna Moralia*. The *Magna Moralia* draws a fundamental contrast between the moral views of Socrates and Plato:

> According . . . to Socrates, all the virtues arise in the reasoning part of the soul (*logistikō tēs psuchēs moriō*); from which it follows that in making the virtues departments of science (*epistēmas*) he ignores our irrational part (*to alogon meros tēs psuchēs*), and thus ignores both passion and the moral character. (1182a18–23)[12]

These views are consistent with Plato's depiction of Socrates in the *Protagoras*, in which we find the single fullest statement of the paradox that all wrongdoing is due to ignorance and of Socrates' moral psychology. In the final argument of this work, the most complete statement of the Socratic position in Plato's early dialogues, Socrates proves the impossibility of *akrasia*, weakness of will. He argues that a person who chooses unwisely in what appears to be the throes of passion actually *chooses* wrongly because of an error in estimating the relative magnitudes of different sources of pleasure. The implication is that knowledge of the art of measuring pleasures and pains would allow people to choose correctly and so would be "the salvation of our life" (*Prt.* 357a).[13]

This reading of the argument in the *Protagoras*—and of Socrates' moral thought in general—is supported by Aristotle's discussion of moral weakness in Book VII of the *Nicomachean Ethics*. He dismisses Socrates' denial of moral weakness out of hand, as inconsistent with the facts of human experience. The view he attributes to Socrates is that "no one acts contrary to what he judges best" (*EN* 1145b34).

Socrates' intellectualist moral psychology has implications that are crucial for understanding his political activity. Because people act according to their opinions as to what is best, to change their opinions is to change their behavior. In the *Apology* he gives a familiar account of the origin of his mission. His associate, Chaerophon, had asked the oracle if anyone were wiser than Socrates (*Ap.* 20e–21a). The negative response surprised Socrates, because he was conscious of being ignorant. Thus he began to use the *elenchos* to inquire into the knowledge of other people in order to ascertain the oracle's meaning. He of course discovered that people knew no more than he did and were deficient in believing that they had knowledge on important subjects. Thus Socrates was wiser than they in possessing distinctive Socratic knowledge of how little he knew. As he says in the *Apology:* "Human wisdom is of little or no value" (23a). The purpose of Socrates' exploration was to discover that on crucial questions of human life only the gods are wise.

However, from the start, Socrates' mission entailed more than merely testing the oracle. It was not enough to have discovered the hollowness of his first subject's claims to knowledge. Socrates then "tried to show him (*epeirōmēn autō deiknunai*) that he thought he was wise but was not" (21c). On his mission, he examines anyone who might claim to be wise, "and when he does not seem so to me, I give aid to the god and show (*endeiknumai*) that he is not wise" (23b). More than simply discovering that people are not wise, Socrates' aim is *to show people* that they are not wise, to puncture their false assurance of moral knowledge, and this as a necessary step to motivating them to begin to think about moral subjects for themselves. Socrates believes that ignorance has pernicious effects in preventing its possessors from seeking moral truth; by puncturing their moral complacency, Socrates believes he can turn them in the proper direction. Discussion of moral subjects with Socrates always has deeper import. As Nicias says in the *Laches:*

> Whoever comes into close contact with Socrates and has any talk with him face to face, is bound to be drawn round and round by him in the course of the argument — though it may have started at first on a quite different theme — and cannot stop until he is led into giving an

account of himself, of the manner in which he now spends his days and of the kind of life he has lived hitherto; and when once he has been led into that, Socrates will never let him go until he has thoroughly and properly put all his ways to the test. (*Lach.* 187e – 88a)

The effect of Socrates' *elenchos* could be powerful. Meno likens it to the sting of the torpedo fish (*Meno* 80a). Socrates dedicated his life to the conviction that the *elenchos*'s sting could turn people onto the path of virtue.

THE TRUE ART OF POLITICS

In the early dialogues, Socrates expresses a number of opinions of the Athenian political system. Most notably, in the *Crito* he argues for a strong account of the citizen's obligation to obey the state. He also expresses criticisms of Athenian democracy. While the Assembly allows only experts to address it on such matters as constructing buildings and outfitting ships, on fundamental matters of state policy all citizens are allowed to speak (*Prt.* 319b – c). This is related to the historical Socrates' well-known criticism of the practice of staffing state offices through the lottery. While one would not choose a shoemaker or a plumber by lot, the people charged with far more important matters of determining state policy and educating the young are chosen this way. Arguments along these lines are found in Xenophon's *Memorabilia* and Aristotle's *Rhetoric* and so can be attributed to the historical Socrates with assurance.[14] More important—and to the point—Socrates categorically criticizes Athenian democracy as corrupt and under the sway of demagogic leaders. Socrates' view of the democracy is no doubt bound up with his high opinion of Sparta.

Interesting as this material is—and Socrates' arguments in the *Crito* are the subject of an entire academic industry—W. K. C. Guthrie is correct in calling Socrates' opinions about the Athenian political system his "political views."[15] His true political teaching must be sought elsewhere. In the *Gorgias* Socrates contrasts his practice with that of the Athenian political leaders—Themistocles, Pericles, Miltiades, and Cimon. Whereas they aim at the mob's gratification, to increase their own power over it,

Socrates pursues "what is best instead of what is most pleasant." He therefore practices "the true art of politics" (*tē . . . alēthōs politikē technē*) (*Grg.* 521d).

One of the great paradoxes of Socrates' political theory—and of Plato's as a whole—is that it is carried out without reference to the existing political system. The Athenian citizenry exhibited a degree of political involvement that is perhaps unprecedented in human history. In his funeral speech in Book II of Thucydides' *History,* Pericles says that the Athenians "do not say that a man who takes no interest in politics is a man who minds his own business; we say that he has no business here at all" (II, 40). However, Socrates pursued his political activity in remove from politics as ordinarily understood. It is true that he performed military service in the Peloponnesian War[16] and at least once served in the Athenian Council, during a particularly tumultuous time (*Ap.* 32a–c). However, his withdrawal from politics is one thing he actually apologizes for (31c). But his reason for this is clear; the mob is irremediably corrupt, and to pursue policies of virtue within the system is a recipe for certain death (31e–32a). Thus he worked in private (*idia; Ap.* 31b, 31c): "I am always busy in your interest, coming to each one of you individually like a father or an elder brother and urging you to care for virtue" (*Ap.* 31b). It was this mission of talking to people, privately, one on one, to which Socrates devoted his life. Although we do not have firm information about how long Socrates busied himself in this pursuit, the fact that Aristophanes featured Socrates as the main character in *The Clouds* bears mention. This play was first performed in 424, by which time Socrates apparently was a recognized Athenian figure and so had probably started talking to people some years before. Thus it appears that Socrates pursued his mission for some thirty years.[17] This is consistent with Socrates' claim in the *Apology* that his mission had reduced him to poverty (31c).

In the *Apology* Socrates says that he practices his elenctic arts indiscriminately. He examines "anyone" (23b), reproaches "each one of you" (31b, 31c). This too is confirmed in the dialogues, as Socrates is depicted as talking to such unpromising characters as Ion and Hippias. While the latter might have been worth arguing with because of his celebrity, at the very end of his life, on the way to his trial, Socrates is depicted as talking with the vain and pompous Euthyphro. Presumably, it would not have taken Socrates long to realize who was and was not a promising candidate for elenctic examination.[18] But he apparently felt duty bound "to give aid to the god" (*Ap.* 23b) and address all of his fellow citizens alike. The solution to the riddle of how Socrates' peculiar, private but indiscriminate activity could be "the only true art of politics" is that he tried to reform his city indirectly by reforming the individuals who constituted it.

We are not able to say how Socrates conceived the final state or condition at which he aimed. The theme of this book is means as opposed to ends. In the case of Socrates, there is good evidence about the former, though for the latter we must rely on speculation. The likeliest view is that Socrates had in mind, simply, a situation in which people were more virtuous and had better values, in which they refrained from injustice and concerned themselves with questions of morality and caring for their souls. I am not sure if this is a sufficiently dramatic break from existing Greek society to be labeled a utopia. But once again Socrates' radicalism was recognized by Callicles: if what Socrates says is true, "must not the life of us human beings have been turned upside down?" (*Grg.* 481c).[19]

However far we are able to go in filling in the aim Socrates sought, for many students of politics, his means of getting there must be viewed as particularly unpromising. To some extent Socrates' activity is more easily defended if we take into account the small size of the Athenian citizenry. Over the course of years, Socrates could conceivably talk to a high percentage of them. Thus if his arguments worked, he could conceivably have succeeded. But this raises the question of how successful he believed individual conversations could be. In the *Crito* he says to Crito that "there are few who believe or ever will believe" his teaching (*Crito* 49d). Thirty years of elenctic activity must have proved disillusioning to Socrates. But whether fortified by genuine hope or only a sense of duty, Socrates pursued this course for decades and refused to withdraw from it even if doing so would save his life (*Ap.* 29d–30a). If the testimony of the dialogues is to be believed, he had staunch faith in his ability to win his interlocutors over to a life of philosophy. In the *Gorgias*—which, as we will see, depicts a great philosophical defeat—he proclaims faith in his method (esp. 474a-b).

Once again, it is important to bear in mind that one reason Socrates was apparently able to retain faith in his method was his unusual account of the psychology of virtue. If virtue is knowledge and there are no non-rational impediments to acting on one's moral convictions, then he who knows what is best will pursue it. If "no one acts contrary to what he judges best" (*EN* 1145b34), then leading people to correct opinions is to turn them on the path of virtue. Socrates believed that ignorance, false conceit of knowledge, was all that stood in the way of reform. Because people think they know what they are doing, they ignore what is truly in their interest and pursue what they think will make them happy. If Socrates could prod them with the gadfly's sting, they could begin to realize the hollowness of their existing beliefs and be turned on the road to moral understanding. Discovering the superior values of caring for the soul and abstaining from injustice should lead them to change their lives. Once again it is impossible to know how successful Socrates believed he would be in this endeavor or what he thought a reformed society would ultimately look like, but he devoted his life to an attempt to effect moral transformation.

THE PLATONIC CRITIQUE

At some point Plato came to believe that Socrates' mission had been fore-doomed to failure. Socrates of course had been executed by the Athenians, and Plato came to see his teacher's fate as evidence of the shortcomings of his strategy. A series of dialogues reveal Plato's deep concern with Socrates' death. The *Apology* of course depicts his defense speeches at this trial, the *Crito* and *Phaedo* his imprisonment and death. Other dialogues mention or allude to his trial and death less directly. But what is less often recognized is that careful reading of these and other dialogues demonstrates an acute understanding of why Socrates failed and suggests a way around his difficulties. The reason this is not widely known, as it seems to me, is that, rather than *discuss* his views directly, in large part Plato *illustrates* them in the dramatic action of several dialogues. Careful reading of the dialogues reveals a record of political failure on the part of Socrates. Only one work depicts an *elenchos* fundamentally affecting a subject, the

Alcibiades I, the authenticity of which is in doubt.[20] For the most part, interlocutors leave the *elenchos* unaffected, while a few become belligerent, even menacing.

Examination of Socrates' unsuccessful encounters reveals Plato's clear understanding of the reasons for this. This recognition is bound up with a fundamental shift in Plato's political theory. I have noted that scholars widely recognize a basic movement in Plato's metaphysical views from the early to the middle dialogues. In the early dialogues, Socrates hunts for the meaning of moral terms. But full answers to his famous "What is X?" questions appear only in the middle dialogues, with the introduction of the theory of Forms. A similar development is apparent in the area of moral psychology, in which the intellectualistic psychology of the early dialogues gives way to the far more realistic tripartite soul. Accompanying these developments is a profound shift in political theory.

My argument here works in two directions. First, we will see that the new political theory of the *Republic* represents decisive criticism and rejection of the political tactics pursued by Socrates on his mission. Thus Plato's own theory of radical reform, put forth in the *Republic,* grows out of recognition of the shortcomings of Socrates' view. I discuss the *Republic* in detail, with special attention to Plato's attempt to overcome problems that defeated Socrates. Second, Plato's very concern with criticizing and rejecting the view of Socrates in an entire series of dialogues is strong evidence for the account of Socrates' views given above. The upshot of the argument here is that Plato, who is often dismissed as utopian, was deeply concerned with practical questions of radical political reform. Not only did he develop his own view through analysis of the flawed view of Socrates, but in doing so, he laid out principles essential to any adequate theory of moral reform.

Perhaps the easiest way to grasp Plato's criticism of Socrates' view is to turn to the opening of the *Republic.* As the dialogue begins, Socrates is walking back from the Piraeus, accompanied by Glaucon, when Polemarchus, Adeimantus, and some other associates catch up with them. The following exchange takes place.

Polemarchus said: It looks to me, Socrates, as if you two are starting off for Athens.

It looks the way it is, then, I said. [Socrates is narrating.]

Do you see how many we are? he said.

I do.

Well you must either prove stronger than we are, or you will have to stay here.

Isn't there another alternative, namely that we persuade you to let us go?

But could you persuade us, if we won't listen?

Certainly not, Glaucon said. (327c)

Though in appearance harmless banter, the situation represented here, Socrates attempting to persuade people who refuse to listen to him, is a recurrent motif in the dialogues and, I would argue, Plato's ironic commentary on the inevitable failure of Socrates' mission.[21]

We can begin with two simple cases. In the *Ion* and the *Euthyphro,* Socrates confronts the vain, obtuse title characters and has little trouble refuting their arguments. When the two figures put forth revised positions, these too give Socrates little trouble. But it is important to note that Socrates' elenctic arguments have little effect, and both figures retreat from the discussions with their beliefs and moral dispositions unaffected. There is nothing startling in these two encounters, although it is somewhat ominous that Socrates meets Euthyphro on his way to address the indictment Meletus has drawn up against him for impiety, while Euthyphro is about to prosecute his father for impiety, for the murder of a slave. The parallel is drawn clearly by Plato (esp. *Euthyph.* 5a–d). Thus the fact that Socrates' arguments do so little to deter Euthyphro from the latter's impious plans does not bode well for Socrates' defense before the Athenian jury.

The failure of the *elenchos* is a more striking feature of the *Philebus.* This late dialogue presents a sophisticated analysis of the value of pleasure. It is interesting to note that the substance of the conversation is between Socrates and Protarchus, who has inherited his part in the argument from Philebus. For the work begins with Philebus *dropping out* of the discussion. Thus an interesting point can be made about the presence of Philebus in this work that bears his name. What is he doing in it? He contributes virtually nothing to the discussion and stands by mute. On the few occasions when he replies to questions, his answers reveal the reason for his presence. Philebus represents a threat (*Phil.* 12a–b). When Protarchus thinks Socrates is guilty of slandering the young, he replies, ostensibly in jest: "[L]et me call your attention Socrates to the fact that there are plenty of us here, all young people. Aren't you afraid that we shall join Philebus in an assault on you, if you keep abusing us?" (16a).[22]

The threat Philebus represents is found in the doctrine he espouses. The pure hedonism he advocates represents a renunciation of reason and as such is immune to logical arguments. Like Callicles (as we shall see), Plato's other advocate of unrestricted hedonism, Philebus can be silenced, but he cannot be convinced.

The truculence of the interlocutor takes on a more overtly menacing aspect in the *Meno*. Whatever the problems with the title character's personality and philosophical abilities, they are overshadowed by the conduct of Anytus, one of the three accusers responsible for bringing Socrates to trial, who joins Socrates and Meno midway in their discussion.[23] When Socrates begins to question him, Anytus bridles at Socrates' (doubtless ironic) proof that the Sophists are the true teachers of civic virtue, although he has had no direct contact with Sophists and is not interested in finding out about them (*Meno* 92b–c). Anytus believes that the Athenian gentry are the true teachers of virtue. When Socrates argues against this view, he becomes angry, even menacing:

> Socrates, I consider you are too apt to speak ill of people. I, for one, if you will take my advice, would warn you to be careful; in most cities it is probably easier to do people harm than good, and particularly in this one; I think you know that yourself. (94e–95a)

With that Anytus leaves, but he is not forgotten. Like other works (the *Charmides* and the *Alcibiades I*), the *Meno* closes on an ominous ironic note. Socrates says to Meno: "It is time now for me to go my way, but do you persuade our friend Anytus of that whereof you yourself are now persuaded, so as to put him in a gentler mood; for if you can persuade him, you will do a good turn to the people of Athens also" (100b). But Anytus of course could not be persuaded.

As noted above, the only example of a successful *elenchos* in the Platonic corpus is found in the *Alcibiades I.* As Paul Friedlander says, only in this dialogue does a character undergo a conversion, "an inner change," in the context of a Platonic work.[24] The genuineness of this dialogue is widely questioned by scholars, although in the absence of conclusive arguments on either side of this question, scholars generally appeal to their negative or positive assessments of the literary quality of the work. On this question I align myself with Friedlander and other scholars who consider the work genuine. In large part, what convinces me is the poignancy of the dialogue, which I attribute to Plato's artistry. In any event the work depicts a protracted dialectical struggle between Socrates and the young title character. But Socrates eventually prevails. As the dialogue ends, Alcibiades has been won over. The *elenchos* has done its work, and Alcibiades vows "to begin here and now to take pains over justice" (*Alc. I* 135d – e). But as I have just noted, the work ends with ironic foreboding; Socrates expresses his apprehension, not from distrust of Alcibiades' nature, "but in view of the might of the state, lest it overcome both me and you" (135e).

The story is resumed in the *Symposium,* by which time Socrates' fears have been realized. Approximately eighteen years have passed since the time depicted in the *Alcibiades I.*[25] The passage of time has shaken the resolve seen at the end of the *Alcibiades I.* Alcibiades has become a politician, of the least scrupulous kind.

In the encomium on Socrates delivered at the end of the *Symposium,* Alcibiades describes the powerful effects of Socrates discourse, which he likens to the power of Marsyas's flute. The *Alcibiades I* depicts this power at work; surprisingly, Alcibiades says that Socrates still affects him.

> Even now I am still conscious that if I consented to lend him my ear, I could not resist him but would have the same feeling again. For he compels me to admit that, sorely deficient as I am, I neglect myself while I attend to the affairs of Athens. (*Symp.* 216a)

But the decision made at the end of the *Alcibiades I* has been overturned. Alcibiades' love of fame and glory — a particular manifestation of the "might of the state" — has proved too much. Alcibiades is the living refutation of Socrates' belief that virtue is knowledge. Although he is aware of the better course, he cannot bring himself to pursue it. Because he knows that he is behaving indefensibly, he is unwilling to talk with Socrates: "So I withhold my ears perforce as from the Sirens, and make off as fast as I can, for fear I should go on sitting beside him till old age was upon me" (216a).

The problem posed by Alcibiades carries us beyond the purview of Socratic ethics. Alcibiades is still susceptible to logical arguments; Socrates can replicate the conversion seen in the *Alcibiades I* at will. But the "inner change" is temporary. Once out of Socrates' sight, Alcibiades is subject to temptations he cannot resist. Because he knows he is doing wrong, he is forced to "take a runaway's leave of [Socrates] and flee away" (216b–c). Clearly, there is something in Alcibiades' psyche over and above the desire to follow the implication of moral principles.

The theme I have traced through this series of dialogues culminates in the *Gorgias,* which depicts the greatest struggle of Socrates' literary life. Problems Socrates has with all three interlocutors, especially Callicles, are so prominent a theme in the work that the evidence cannot be discussed in detail here.[26] For anyone familiar with the *Gorgias,* a moment's reflection indicates the significance of this theme. It is particularly striking that in his climactic struggle with Callicles, Socrates explicitly says that he does not speak only for himself but for philosophy as well (*Grg.* 482a–b). As Callicles falls silent, impervious to Socrates' questions, the dramatic action of the work illustrates the impotence of philosophy, in a context in which Plato sketches an outline of the mature political theory of the *Republic.*[27]

Because of the wealth of relevant material in the *Gorgias,* I will merely sketch aspects of Socrates' encounter with Callicles. What is especially important for our purposes is that on Callicles' entry into the discussion, Socrates expostulates at considerable length on the commitments of dialectic, which Callicles has by implication accepted in joining the discussion. In such a discussion, both parties are bound to accept the conclusions that emerge (481c–82c, 486d–88b). In this case, a set of moral precepts had emerged in the earlier discussions with Gorgias and Polus. If Callicles is unable to refute them, he too is bound to accept them (482b–c). But in his response Callicles distinguishes the world of the discussion, which is the philosopher's realm of argument, from the world outside.

> So when they [philosophers] enter upon any private or public busi-
> ness they make themselves ridiculous, just as on the other hand, I
> suppose, when public men engage in your studies and discussions,
> they are quite ridiculous. (484d–e)

Callicles does not expect to prevail in the debate. But this is of little concern to him, because he cares little for the domain of argument. He is interested in the world outside the discussion, and it is this world that he
advises Socrates to heed. The discussion means little to him, because he
can always walk away from it. And if he walks away unconvinced, Socrates
may have won the debate proper, but the *elenchos* will have failed.

The only way Socrates can win over Callicles is if he can get him to
accept the commitments of dialectic. Socrates lays out the necessary procedures for the debate and insists that the only standard of truth is mutual
agreement (487d–e). Although the conclusions that emerge might not be
true in any ultimate sense, they are the best possible for now and must be
accepted as true until better arguments can be found to replace them.
Socrates declares that he and Callicles should live their lives in accordance with the results of the argument (488a–b).

The discussion itself gives Socrates little trouble. Within a few questions, he has Callicles contradicting himself. But the latter responds with
an angry outburst: "What an inveterate driveller the man is! Tell me, are
you not ashamed to be wordcatching at your age, and if one makes a ver-
bal slip, to take that as a stroke of luck" (489b–c).

Callicles shifts his ground and the discussion continues. As he is
trapped by the *elenchos,* he repeatedly changes his position, with Socrates
upbraiding him for doing so (491b–c). But Callicles eventually bridles
under the dialectical assault:

> CALLICLES: I cannot follow these subtleties of yours, Socrates.
> SOCRATES: You can, but you play the innocent, Callicles. Just go on a
>   little further . . .
> CALLICLES: I cannot tell what you mean. (497a–b)

At this point Gorgias must intervene. It is only at his insistence that the discussion continues, with Callicles saying: "Well then, proceed with those little cramped questions of yours, since Gorgias is so minded" (497b–c).

This last exchange is revealing. Although Callicles can be induced to continue, the debate means nothing to him, and it is only in realization of this that he allows it to go on. He answers Socrates mechanically, shifting his position each time he is trapped, but even this degree of cooperation will not last long.

> CALLICLES: Why not name it yourself, Socrates?
> SOCRATES: Well, if you prefer it, I will; and do you, if I seem to you
> to name it rightly say so; if not, you must refute me and not let
> me have my way. (504c)

Socrates carries on virtually alone. At the conclusion of each lengthy question, he asks, "Is this true?" "Yes or no?" or something similar, and Callicles mechanically yields an affirmative response. But he tires of even this degree of cooperation: "I have no idea what you are referring to, Socrates; do ask someone else" (505c). Socrates' repeated pleas that the discussion be allowed to continue fall on deaf ears: "How overbearing you are, Socrates! Take my advice and let this argument drop, or find someone else to argue with" (505d).

Socrates is forced to continue the argument alone, responding to his own questions. At one point this cruel parody of dialectic appears to have the desired effect on Callicles: "It seems to me, I cannot tell how, that your statement is right, Socrates, but I share the common feeling. I do not quite believe you" (513c). Socrates knows the reason for this: "Because the love of Demos, Callicles, is there in your soul to resist me . . ." (513c). As in the case of Alcibiades, the force of Socrates' arguments must do battle in their subject's soul with the love of power and acclaim.

Callicles' weakening is temporary (514e–15a), and the pattern that dominates his encounter with Socrates reasserts itself. Callicles is entrenched in his views, although he can neither defend them nor criticize Socrates' position. Although, as Socrates says, the argument stands firm, "fastened . . . with reasons of steel and adamant" (509a), and Callicles cannot begin to undo this chain, it has no effect on him. As the dialogue concludes, Callicles' choice of how he is going to live is the same as it has always been. He will pursue a political life (521a–b), and he has no defense of his position except that Socrates' way of life may one day result in his being tried on some false charge, with dire consequences (521c).

If we conclude that Plato has carefully worked the failure of Socrates' elenctic mission into the dramatic action of many dialogues, the question of course is exactly what this means. To begin with, it seems that Plato's dramatic critique of the Socratic *elenchos* is similar to the view expressed by Aristotle, in Book X of the *Nicomachean Ethics*.

There, having thoroughly analyzed what virtue is, Aristotle turns to the question of how people can be made virtuous. One possibility he considers is the view of Socrates that people can be made good through persuasion alone.[28] But he criticizes this view for much the same reason he rejects Socrates' view of moral weakness: it conflicts with obvious facts.

> Now if discourses on ethics were sufficient in themselves to make men virtuous, "large fees and many" (as Theognis says) "would they win," quite rightly, and to provide such discourses would be all that is wanted. But as it is, we see that although they have power to stimulate and encourage generous youths, and, given an inborn nobility of character and a genuine love of what is noble, can make them susceptible to the influence of virtue, yet they are powerless to stimulate the mass of mankind to moral nobility. (*EN* 1179b4–10)

Aristotle believes that people's conduct is heavily influenced by their psychological dispositions, largely established during childhood. Accordingly: "What argument can reform the natures of men like these? To dislodge by arguments habits long firmly rooted in their characters is difficult if not impossible" (1179b16–18). Reason works only on those who have been made susceptible through proper upbringing. People who have not been raised properly must be reformed through other means (1179b23 ff.). Because people are made good mainly through habituation, the young must be brought up according to good laws, in properly governed *poleis* (1179b31 ff.). If such matters are neglected by the *polis*, the individual should do whatever he can. Given the foregoing, he will be most effective if he makes himself skilled in legislation (1180a24–34). This is the transition from Aristotle's *Ethics* to his *Politics*.

I believe that by the time he wrote the *Republic,* Plato had come to have a view of Socrates' method similar to that of Aristotle. This is the ironic message of the dramatic defeats we have reviewed, while as we have seen, a broad hint in this direction is given on the opening page of the *Republic.*

In the middle dialogues, especially the *Republic,* Plato has a new conception of virtue, based on the tripartite soul. In addition to knowledge— or true belief—concerning what is right, virtue requires a proper ordering of the parts of the soul. Only if reason "rules" will the individual be able to ward off the promptings of appetite and do what is right. The departure Plato's recognition of the importance of the appetitive parts of the soul represents from Socratic moral psychology is recognized in the *Magna Moralia,* as seen above.

The new moral psychology of the *Republic* and other middle dialogues requires a new conception of how people are made virtuous.[29] The appetitive parts, which dominate the soul, must be conditioned to be harmonious with and subordinate to reason. Plato firmly believes that the soul is most malleable in early childhood and so that the necessary conditioning must occur during people's early years. This view of course bears fruit in the great attention he pays to early education. It is no exaggeration to say that the political theory of the *Republic* is based on harnessing all possible resources of the city to make sure that the young are educated properly. The details here are too familiar to require discussion. But Plato advocates a completely controlled environment; all artistic media are to be carefully censored.

> We must seek out such artists as have the talent to pursue the beautiful and the graceful in their work, in order that our young men shall be benefited from all sides like those who live in a healthy place, whence something from these beautiful works will strike their eyes and ears like a breeze that brings health from salubrious places, and lead them unawares from childhood to love of, resemblance to, and harmony with, the beauty of reason. (*Rep.* 401c–d)

Upbringing of this sort will make people sensitive to order and harmony and so temperance and justice while they are still young, before they are able to understand the reasons. When they are older, they will recognize and welcome the reasons (401d–2a).

Only if this is done will the young be virtuous. In reading the *Republic*, it is well to keep in mind the more extreme view advanced in the *Laws*. In his last work, Plato argues that in order to be made virtuous, people must be educated from before birth. Pregnant women are to perform rhythmic exercises, to instill rhythm and harmony in the souls of the unborn babies (*Laws* 798a–e). The distance between this and the Socratic view of moral education is vividly conveyed by John Gould in his work, *The Development of Plato's Ethics*, which juxtaposes the views put forth in the Socratic dialogues and the *Laws*.[30] I believe it can be shown that the new Platonic view, argued for most directly in Book IV of the *Republic*, is advanced in explicit criticism and rejection of Socratic moral psychology. But that is not necessary here.[31] However much Plato had the deficiencies of Socratic ethics explicitly in mind, he recognized that his new conception of moral education required a new political approach. Proper conditioning of the souls of the young requires control of the environment. The philosopher cannot stand apart from the political process but must dominate it in order to be able to shape the educational environment. In other words, the philosopher must also be king.

Plato's political theory in the *Republic* is built around this set of connections. Other notorious institutions that Plato recommends, notably community of the family and of property, are secondary, intended to make sure that the philosophers do not abuse their power. As Plato says in Book IV, as long as the system of education is preserved, all will go well, and the citizens will improve with each generation (423e–24b).

Given his new moral psychology, Plato can clearly see the problems with Socrates' tactics of moral reform. As I have shown, this realization is woven into the dramatic action of an entire series of dialogues. In Book VI of the *Republic*, Plato directly discusses the impotence of the philosopher in a corrupt city. The force of the environment decisively shapes the souls of all inhabitants. In attempting to shape the soul of even a single inhabitant, the philosopher would be combating the force of the entire environment. Even the best, most gifted characters would resist his prompt-ings: "There is not now, has not been in the past, nor will ever be in the future, a man of a character so unusual that he has been educated to vir-tue in spite of the education he received from the mob" (492e).

As the philosopher is unable to win over individual citizens, he fares no better in confronting society as a whole. In the analogy of the Cave, Plato describes what would happen if the prisoner, who had been freed from the cave and seen the light, were to return to rescue his former fellow prisoners: "As for the man who tried to free them and lead them upward, if they could somehow lay their hands on him and kill him, they would do so" (517a).

Given these circumstances, the philosophers must withdraw from politics. They should not take part in governing their cities, nor should they pursue the private politics of a Socratic mission. The true philoso-pher "keeps quiet and minds his own business."

> Like a man who takes refuge under a small wall from a storm of dust or hail driven by the wind, and seeing other men filled with lawless-ness, the philosopher is satisfied if he can somehow live his present life free from injustice and impious deeds and depart from it with a beautiful hope, blameless and content. (496d–e)

If he wants to reform his city, or specific inhabitants, the philosopher must become philosopher-king.

C H A P T E R   T H R E E

The Politics of Philosophy

In the *Republic* Plato moves beyond criticizing Socrates to presenting a developed alternative view. Though, again, Plato is generally dismissed as a utopian theorist, I argue that he was quite
serious about establishing the ideal city of the *Republic*—or some
similacrum—and explored how this could be done. It is important to examine Plato's position here; he addresses timeless
problems confronting any would-be radical reformer and in fact
does so with the dispassionate logic that characterizes his political theory as a whole. Also, Plato's inquiries into the political theory of radical reform are of a piece with political activities
throughout his life.

THE POLITICAL THEORY OF RADICAL REFORM

To assess Plato's view of radical reform, we must examine his
views on the way political reform should unfold and then practical questions concerning the possibility of reforming actual cities.
To begin with the former, Plato is unequivocal about the need for
radical reform. In his view a city's overall environment decisively
shapes the souls of its inhabitants. He does not systematically
examine the factors that determine a city's overall spirit—akin to

"general spirit," in Montesquieu's sense.[1] Plato probably believed that they varied from place to place. But in a city that is well governed, these matters are not left to chance. Through an exercise of will, they can be controlled and the populace molded according to a definite pattern. In Book I of the *Laws* the Athenian Stranger praises Sparta for self-consciously educating the young according to an idea of virtue, although he criticizes the particular conception of virtue pursued there. In the just city, proper education, especially in childhood, takes precedence over all else. Proper education can create a margin of safety for dealing with problems when they arise and compensate for other shortcomings (*Rep.* 423e–24b). If it is futile to attempt to educate even a single individual against the many's conception of virtue, everything possible must be done to make sure that a correct conception of virtue is inculcated through education: "[W]hen children play the right games from the beginning and absorb lawfulness from music and poetry, it follows them in everything and fosters their growth, correcting anything in the city that may have gone wrong before" (*Rep.* 425a).

The implication here is that reform must be total. It is useless to tinker with specific institutions in order to attempt to improve things. The all-embracing spirit of the city will turn any changes attempted back toward the original spirit. And so Plato does not discuss specific regulations about such matters as market business and private contracts. If the city as a whole is well governed, these matters will take care of themselves. If it is not, specific laws will not help; changes will be corrupted immediately. Reformers "will spend their lives enacting a lot of other laws and then amending them," believing that in this way they will improve things (425e). But improvement is not possible without fundamental change of "the city's whole political establishment (*katastasin tes poleōs olēn*)" (426b–c). Plato likens people who attempt to reform a city through specific changes to doctors who treat a patient's symptoms without getting to the licentiousness and other bad habits that are responsible for his condition in the first place (425e–26b). To pass laws on specific matters in hopes of reform is to attempt to cut off a Hydra's heads (426e).

In the *Republic* Plato takes this line of argument to its logical conclusion. If successful reform requires institution of proper educational measures, then he recommends directing all the resources of the state toward proper education. As we have seen, this requires censorship of all artistic media in an environment that is completely controlled. The question of establishing a proper educational environment is faced forthrightly. To overcome the (literally) demoralizing effects of the previously corrupt environment, upon attaining political power the philosophers must clean the canvas of the state:

> They'd take the city and the characters of human beings as their sketching slate, but first they'd wipe it clean—which isn't at all an easy thing to do. And you should know that this is the plain difference between them and others, namely, that they refuse to take either an individual or a city in hand or to write laws, unless they receive a clean slate or are allowed to clean it themselves. (501a)

At the end of Book VII, Plato discusses how the slate is to be cleaned. All inhabitants of the city over the age of ten will be sent into the country: "Then [the philosophers] will take possession of the children who are now free from the ethos of their parents, and bring them up in their own customs and laws, which are the ones we've described" (541a). This is "the quickest and easiest way" for the city to be established on the right foot (541a).

One cannot but be struck by the casual brutality of Plato's proposals, and commentators have long questioned his seriousness in advancing them, a subject to which I will return. But as the solution to a political problem, Plato's ideas are convincing on one level. If the existing order is corrupt and so deforming the souls of the young, then it must be eliminated.

Probably the most celebrated critic of Plato's political theory is Karl Popper, in volume I of *The Open Society and Its Enemies.*[2] Popper presents important general criticisms of what he calls "utopian engineering," which he believes to apply to Plato.[3] The attempt to remold society as a whole is a gigantic undertaking. Such an endeavor requires that the would-be reformer start out with a complete blueprint of the planned society. However, as plans are put into practice, the need to make changes will be apparent, although if too much is changed, the plan is effectively jettisoned. On the other hand, wholesale reform will inconvenience many people for a protracted time. To deal with their resistance, the reformer requires considerable power, but this of course can be easily abused, giving rise to a dictatorship. In contrast to wholesale reform, Popper presents his own favored method, which he describes as "piecemeal social engineering." Popper is especially interested in the need to learn about what does and does not work in society through a process of trial and error. The piecemeal method centers on social experimentation, combating identifiable evils, learning from the experience and moving on to deal with additional evils, and so on. But for the utopian engineer, this sort of learning process is short-circuited. To deal with the opposition that large-scale projects invite, the reformer will suppress criticism, including reasonable criticism. Necessary corrections will not be made, causing things to go farther astray, which will generate increased opposition, and so on. Thus Popper sees attempts at utopian engineering ending up as dictatorial societal disasters — evils that can be avoided through a one-step-at-a-time, trial-and-error method.

But Plato has a powerful argument against piecemeal reform. The problems with existing society are on a fundamental moral level. The environment is corrupt and replicates itself in the souls of each succeeding generation. Tinkering with specific components of the system is futile, because the all-embracing social spirit will impress itself on new institutions, as it has on the old. Reforming the moral substance of a community is different from working one's way toward a nationwide health system that will cover all Americans, or a social welfare program that really works. One of Plato's central political beliefs is that a city's environment contains a comprehensive moral substance that shapes everything after it. To leave this unaffected guarantees that things will not really change.

In another respect as well, Popper's analysis does not address Plato's central concerns. Plato is insistent that the philosopher-rulers work to improve the state over time. They are to keep an open mind on questions of policy and so address criticisms of their handiwork. This requirement extends to central features of the city. For instance, the philosophers must be willing to examine the treatment of poetry, which is fundamental and the subject of detailed discussion throughout the *Re-*

public, should poets or other defenders of poetry argue against Plato's proposals (*Rep.* 607c ff.).[4]

To become clearer on Plato's position in the *Republic,* I return to the theme of educational realism. Educational realism refers to the difficulty of inculcating specific, desired personality traits in a subject population and corresponding difficulties in reorienting those that have been established already. Because psychological dispositions are complex and deep-seated, protracted conditioning must play a significant role in their establishment. We have seen that Socrates denied the force of educational realism, and Aristotle criticized him for this: "To dislodge by arguments habits long firmly rooted in [people's] characters is difficult if not impossible" (*EN* 1179b16–18).

Plato, in contrast, addresses the problem of educational realism head-on. He is clearly influenced by the example of Sparta—the model in Book VIII for the best of the inferior states. But Plato takes things much farther. Other important political thinkers have shared Plato's belief in the power of the environment to condition its inhabitants, although Plato is perhaps alone in the amount of influence he attributes to artistic media. At the risk of hyperbole, I would assert that in the history of western political theory no other thinker, certainly no other major thinker, pursues the implications of this belief so clearly to their logical conclusion. Once again, a central tenet of Plato's political theory is that everything possible must be done to inculcate virtue. The possibilities are bounded by the limitations of human nature. The three-class system is required by fundamental differences in the makeup of different people. But with this fact kept firmly in mind, everything possible is done to raise each group of people to the highest level of virtue it can attain.

Plato also goes beyond the Spartan model in believing that successful reform requires a clean break with the existing order. The existing inhabitants must be sent into the country while the next generation is educated properly. Unlike Lycurgus, Plato deals directly with the problem of "the first generation." The existing generation, corrupt as they are, must somehow be induced to accept new institutions, which represent a sharp break with existing society. I have discussed how Lycurgus and Solon achieved the requisite power—and I will turn directly to Plato's thoughts on this matter. But more than affecting merely the possibility of realizing reform, the problem of the first generation involves the threat of contamination. Even if the existing generation is willing to accept reform, their presence could decisively interfere with its consummation. Having been raised under corrupt conditions, they will pass their corruption on, unless strong measures are taken to prevent this. We do not find discussion of this issue in our account of Sparta (see above, p. 17). Perhaps in that case the new institutions alone were able to effect the necessary break with existing society. Or perhaps Plato's truly radical proposal arose from his realization that the kind of virtue he pursues breaks more sharply with existing society than did Spartan military virtue and so requires stronger measures. But once again Plato ruthlessly follows the implications of his argument to their logical conclusion. Thus alongside his "educational realism" we can place his "generational realism," his recognition that even if fundamental reforms are enacted, drastic measures must be taken to prevent the existing, corrupt generation from throwing the process off track.

PHILOSOPHERS AND KINGS

If the philosophers require complete control of the environment to enact the necessary reforms, we must look into the means through which they are to attain this. Plato addresses this question through the paradox of the philosopher-king. The paradox is familiar, but it is worthwhile to quote it here:

> Until philosophers rule as kings or those who are now called kings and leading men genuinely and adequately philosophize, that is, until political power and philosophy entirely coincide, while the many natures who at present pursue either one exclusively are forcibly prevented from doing so, cities will have no rest from evils. (473c–d)

As Plato says elsewhere, "at whatever time the muse of philosophy controls a city," the constitution Socrates and his interlocutors have been describing will exist (499c–d).

The paradox presents two different ways in which the muse of philosophy can come to power. Either philosophers can become kings or kings can become philosophers. Although once the city has been established it will not matter which of the two was pursued, it is important to note that two entirely different sets of political problems are involved. Transforming a philosopher into a king entails the impediments an individual or group of individuals must overcome to attain power. Transforming a king into a philosopher involves convincing one man who already has power that he should follow the path of philosophy. Although both paths are unpromising, it is interesting that Plato avoids the former in favor of the latter, although this provides in essence no hope.

In the *Republic* Plato does not discuss means through which philosophers can gain power. In the absence of discussion, it is not possible to say why. But it seems that in this regard, biographical considerations could well be important. In his autobiographical *Seventh Epistle,* Plato recounts his early experiences in Athenian politics, in the tumultuous years at the end of the Peloponnesian War. He recounts how members of the Thirty Tyrants were his relatives and associates and invited him to join them "in what seemed to be a proper undertaking." But his hopes that this new government would lead the city in the direction of justice were disappointed, as its rule became far worse than the previous constitution (*Ep.* 7 324c–e). His disillusionment was increased when the restored democracy committed the unforgivable sin of prosecuting and executing Socrates (324d–25c). As Plato contemplated the corruption of Athenian laws and customs, he eventually concluded that "all existing states are badly governed and the condition of their laws practically incurable, without some miraculous remedy and the assistance of fortune" (325c–26a). The miraculous remedy was the idea of the philosopher-king.

> I was forced to say, in praise of true philosophy, that from her height alone was it possible to discern what the nature of justice is, either in the state or in the individual, and that the ills of the human race would never end until those who are sincerely and truly lovers of wisdom come into political power, or the rulers of our cities, by the grace of God, learn true philosophy. (326a–b)

The terms in which this is stated are similar to what is seen in the *Republic*. It is notable—and important for the overall argument here—that Plato came to this conclusion when he was still a young man, long before he wrote the *Republic*. I return to the implications of this point below. To my mind, it seems likely that the horrors of the Thirty's rule by force that Plato witnessed discouraged him from pursuing this path in the *Republic*. He expresses repugnance at the use of political violence later in the *Epistle*. He says that one should warn his city, if he thinks there is a chance he will be listened to and this will not put him in danger of his life. But if persuasion will not work,

> let him not use violence upon his fatherland to bring about a change of constitution. If what he thinks is best can only be accomplished by the exile and slaughter of men, let him keep his peace and pray for the welfare of himself and his city. (*Ep.* 7 331c–d)

On the basis of these two points, one can well understand why Plato does not pursue the possibility of having the philosopher attempt to seize power. But as is often the case with Plato, there is also contradictory evidence. In the *Statesman* he argues that the ideal ruler, informed by philosophic insight, is justified in using force against his city.[5] In addition, as we will see below, Plato was involved in the attempt by his friend and associate, Dion, to seize power in Syracuse—then the most powerful city in the Greek world. One can identify differences between the situations envisioned in the *Statesman* and in regard to Dion and that confronting the philosopher intent on ascending to power.[6] But whether or not this explanation is persuasive, in the *Republic* Plato does not address the possibility of philosophers rising to power, preferring to place his hopes in kings becoming philosophers.

However, this position leaves Plato with little hope of ever seeing the just city realized. Rather than attempt to demonstrate that this eventuality is likely or even possible, Plato is content to argue that it is not impossible, and this "in the whole of time." The argument itself is in three simple steps. First, it is not impossible that children of kings can be born with philosophical natures. Second and less likely, it is not inevitable that such children will be corrupted. Although it is hard for even one to be saved, this is not impossible (502a–b). Then if this ruler institutes laws and practices of the kind described in the dialogue, it is not impossible that the citizenry will be willing to comply (502b). It does strain one's credulity to imagine that the inhabitants of a city would be willing to go out to the country and leave their children to be raised by the philosophers. But Plato is perhaps correct that it is not impossible—in the wholeness of time. Thus he concludes that "this legislation is best if only it is possible, and that, while it is hard for it to come about, it is not impossible" (502c).

This conclusion is asserted in several contexts in the *Republic*. In Book VI: "Since it is not impossible for this to happen, we are not speaking of impossibilities. That it is difficult for it to happen, however, we agree ourselves" (499d). At the end of Book VII: "Then, do you agree that the things we've said about the city and its constitution aren't altogether wishful thinking, that it's hard for them to come about, but not impossible?" (540d). In a celebrated passage at the end of Book IX, Plato is widely believed to have renounced the possibility of the just city, or to have admitted his lack of seriousness about actual reform.[7] But if one looks more closely, one will see that the message of this passage is essentially no different. Socrates closes the Book by remarking that the city he and his interlocutors have been describing exists in theory, though not anywhere on earth. Then Socrates says:

> But perhaps, I said, there is a model of it in heaven, for anyone who wants to look at it and to make himself its citizen on the strength of what he sees. It makes no difference whether it is or ever will be somewhere, for he would take part in the practical affairs of that city and no other. (592a–b)

This passage appears to be more pessimistic in tone than the ones we have seen. However, we should note that Plato does not here express indifference as to whether the just city is ever realized. The immediate question under discussion is whether the just man will take part in politics (591e). Socrates declares that he will, "at least in his own kind of city. But he may not be willing to do so in his fatherland, unless some divine good luck chances to be his" (592a). As noted above, although the just city is "difficult but not impossible," its realization depends on a series of unlikely eventualities, each dependent on the ones that have gone before, which collectively constitute "divine good luck." But if the hoped-for circumstances do not arise, the philosopher will not take part in politics in an ordinary city. The passage adds to what we have seen only that in the absence of divine good fortune, the philosopher will serve only in the replica of the just city constructed in his soul.

Further evidence of Plato's seriousness about the possibility of transforming a king into a philosopher is provided by his experiences in Sicily. What transpired is recounted in the *Seventh Epistle* and need not be reviewed in detail here. Briefly, when he was about sixty years of age, Plato was alerted to the possibility of turning Dionysius II, the young tyrant of Syracuse, in the direction of philosophy. The *Epistles* do not say exactly what Plato hoped to accomplish in Syracuse. Although it is unlikely that he ever hoped to convert Dionysius into a full-fledged philosopher-king, he remarks that success at his endeavor "would mean an incalculably blessed life for the tyrant himself and the other Syracusans" (*Ep.* 7 327c). The evidence of *Epistle 8* as well as *Epistle 7* suggests that Plato hoped to bring about reforms in Syracuse along the lines of the "second best" city described in the *Laws*. Several considerations support this possibility.[8] First, scholars have noted that the institutions described in the *Laws*, especially the earlier books, seem devised with Sicily in mind. In addition, there are close resemblances between the institutions described in the *Laws* and those Plato recommends for Syracuse in *Epistle 8*.[9] Finally and most intriguingly, although the city described in the *Laws* is a new colony that is to be set up by the Cnossians, with Cleinias as one of the lawgivers (702b–d), Plato inexplicably presents another means of implementing the city. If the lawgiver could join forces with a willing monarch, that would be the quickest and easiest way of bringing the second best state into existence (709c–12b). Plato's appeal to a monarch who is young, intelligent, and virtuous (709e–10a) cannot but recall the hopes he had harbored for Dionysius II. That Plato segues into a discussion of this topic when the city in the *Laws* is to be established as a colony of Cnossos is puzzling.

Whatever we decide about the relationship between the *Laws* and Plato's plans in regard to Syracuse, it is clear that he became embroiled in

Syracusan politics. Dion pleaded with Plato to put his theories of political reform into practice. If the desire for virtuous rule could be roused in Dionysius, "a true and happy life" could be established without violent upheaval (327d): "What better opportunity can we expect," he said, "than the situation which Providence has presented us with?" (327e). Although Plato was not hopeful, knowing the flightiness of the young, he decided to make the attempt. The decisive consideration, he reports, was shame "lest I appear to myself as a pure theorist, unwilling to touch any practical task" (328c).

After the fashion of Socrates, Plato attempted to win Dionysius over with philosophical arguments, although he apparently did not try the Socratic *elenchos*. Instead, it seems that he devoted the major part of his efforts to establishing the sort of relationship with Dionysius that was necessary for successful persuasion (see 331d–33a, 340b–41a, 345a–b). But Dionysius proved unworthy of Plato's efforts and the mission failed — opening the way for the tragic events that followed. Dion led an invasion of Syracuse. This succeeded for a time, but in the tumult of civil war, Dion could do little more than attempt to cling to power, until he was assassinated, by Callipus, a member of Plato's Academy.

Little definite can be said about the significance of these events for understanding Plato's political theory in the *Republic*. Perhaps they support Plato's apparent decision in the *Republic* not to pursue political reform through violence. Whether or not we accept this contention, it is natural to connect tragic events in Sicily with Plato's decisive rejection of violent means in *Epistle* 7 and his later political theory. Scholars hold different views about Plato's abortive adventures in Sicily. John Burnet, for example, says that there "was nothing chimerical in the project" and that had Plato succeeded, he might have done for Syracuse what the Pythagorean philosopher, Lysis, did for Thebes in educating Epaminondas. But other scholars are more critical. W. K. C. Guthrie, for example, says it is not surprising that the author of the *Republic* and *Laws* proved "something of a political innocent," out of place in the rough-and-tumble of political life.[10] But questions as to whether Plato was out of his depth should be kept distinct from questions concerning his intentions. I return to the latter, in reference to his political activities in connection with the Academy, below.

PLATO AND RADICAL REFORM

The highly politicized account of Plato's political theory discussed to this point is widely disputed in the literature. Scholarly opinion on this issue has fluctuated over the last century. Toward the end of the nineteenth century and the beginning of the twentieth, scholars generally subscribed to what I will call the "traditional" view that Plato was deeply concerned with actual moral reform in the dialogues. For example, this view is expressed by Ernest Barker, in his classic work, *Greek Political Theory: Plato and His Predecessors,* first published in 1918 but still the standard work on Plato's political theory. According to Barker, it is impossible to read the *Republic*—and other works of Plato—"without believing that political reform was the pre-occupation of Plato's mind."[11] Among authors expressing similar views are R. L. Nettleship, Hans Raeder, T. A. Sinclair, and F. M. Cornford, although none of these scholars goes into the matter in much detail or carries his analysis much beyond Plato's discussion in *Republic VI,* as seen above.[12] But more recently scholarly opinion has turned. Views—to which I will refer as "nonpolitical"—are currently far more widespread. According to the nonpolitical interpretation, the *Republic* is not meant to contain practical political proposals. Scholars support this contention on two basic grounds: (a) the ostensible structure of the argument in the *Republic;* and (b) the impracticability of many of Plato's proposals for the ideal state. These objections can be discussed in turn, though I will focus more attention on (b).[13]

To begin with (a), there is no question that the *Republic* is at least ostensibly a discussion of justice and that this discussion informs the structure of the work. It is to meet the challenge of Glaucon and Adeimantus that Socrates raises the question of the ideal city. Since justice in the city is larger and easier to discern than justice in the soul, Socrates constructs the just city in order to illumine the just soul (368c – 69a). Because the *Republic* is an inquiry into the nature of justice and the topic of the just city is said to have been introduced to further this aim, scholars have argued that Plato is not serious about his political proposals, that *the* theme of the work is justice, not political reform. A typical expression of this view is given by Guthrie:

[T]he truth is that Plato is not devising a society with a view to its ever coming into being. He is telling us what it would be like *if* philosophers came to power, not because he seriously believes that they will, but in order to reveal his conception of human nature at its best, or in his phraseology, "justice in the individual."[14]

I do not find this view convincing. To begin with, it seems strained to argue that a given Platonic dialogue must have *one* theme and so that if no other theme is *the* theme of the work, these other themes should be taken less seriously. Many dialogues touch on different themes. To cite perhaps the clearest example, the *Gorgias* presents in-depth explorations of both the moral life *and* rhetoric. The work is not *about* one or the other but of course about both.[15] In the *Gorgias,* as often in the dialogues, Plato's discussion of one of his themes serves to broaden and deepen his treatment of the others. This kind of reciprocal enhancement is basic to Plato's technique.

There are additional reasons. Even if the *Republic* is ostensibly an examination of the nature of justice, to which discussion of the just city is subordinate, Plato finds it necessary to depart from this structure. The discussion of justice is carried on only in Books I and II–IV and VIII–IX. Books V–VII, in which, not incidentally, Plato touches on his deepest philosophical truths, are formally an interlude, a digression prompted by the interruption of the interlocutors, who raise three great "waves" of criticism, including "the biggest and most difficult one," whether it is possible for the just city to exist and how this can be accomplished (472c ff.). The fact that Plato departs from discussing justice directly in these crucial books does considerable damage to the contention that the city is discussed *only* for this purpose. Nor do I agree with Julia Annas's claim that Plato says "little about the city except in so far as concerns its justice."[16] The detailed accounts of the treatment of women and the community of the family, in addition to implementing the city, are far more than the discussion of justice requires — to say nothing of the highly specific discussion of education in the arts in Books II and III. In general, Plato's description of the just city is far too detailed to be justified solely on the basis of what is needed for the argument that justice pays.[17]

A more difficult case is presented by scholars who argue that aspects of the just city are so wildly impractical that Plato could not have intended them seriously. An often cited example is Plato's proposal for rusticating the population. I. M. Crombie and Gerald Levinson, to name two scholars, adduce this proposal as evidence that, politically speaking, Plato could not be serious.[18] This line of argument is most familiarly associated with Leo Strauss and Allan Bloom and scholars influenced by them. In his "Interpretive Essay" on the *Republic,* Bloom writes:

> Socrates [i.e., the Socrates of the *Republic*] constructs his utopia to point up the dangers of what we would call utopianism; as such it is the greatest critique of political idealism ever written. . . . The striving for the perfectly just city puts unreasonable and despotic demands on ordinary men, and it abuses and misuses the best men. There is gentleness in Socrates' treatment of men, and his vision is never clouded by the blackness of moral indignation, for he knows what to expect of men. Political idealism is the most destructive of human passions.[19]

Similarly, according to Strauss: "Certain it is that the *Republic* supplies the most magnificent cure ever devised for every form of political ambition."[20]

The view of Bloom and Strauss cannot easily be discussed in isolation from their views concerning how Plato's texts should be interpreted.[21] Most striking is their belief that great significance should be attributed to apparently minor details in the texts they examine. I quote Bloom:

> [In Plato's dialogues e]very word has its place and its meaning, and when one cannot with assurance explain any detail, he can know that his understanding is incomplete. When something seems boring or has to be explained away as a convention, it means that the interpreter has given up and has taken his place among the ranks of those Plato intended to exclude from the center of his thought.[22]

Taken in one sense, what Bloom says is trivially true. One has not understood a Platonic work *entirely* unless one understands every detail. But Bloom's implication is far more radical: one has not understood a Platonic work *at all,* that is, one has not understood its true meaning (the "center" of Plato's thought), unless one understands every detail. This principle is highly questionable. It rests on a number of assumptions about the nature of Plato's texts that, to the best of my knowledge, have never been adequately defended. Considerable evidence would have to be produced to demonstrate that Plato elaborately hid the true meaning of his works from all but those able to unravel their apparently minor details.

Setting aside this issue of interpretation, I wish to examine the claim that central institutions of the *Republic* are so clearly absurd that Plato could not have been serious in presenting them. To substantiate this claim, it is important to bear in mind that more than the fact that the institutions are unworkable must be demonstrated. Rather it must be shown that Plato believed they would not work. In other words, the institutions must be shown to be unworkable even if we grant basic premises and assumptions of Plato's political theory. The key premise is Plato's great faith in the plasticity of human nature and the power of education. Institutions and practices that might appear to be impossible under ordinary conditions would take on quite a different cast if men's passions and desires were ordered differently. Unless strong evidence could be brought forward against Plato's commitment to these premises, they must be taken into account in assessing the institutions.

To illustrate the shortcomings of Strauss's and Bloom's strategy, we can look at Plato's recommendation concerning the treatment of women and the family. In a 1977 article responding to a critic, Bloom examines the absurdity of Plato's proposed equality of women.[23] Plato's proposals are absurd, Bloom contends, because of the humorousness of seeing men and women exercising naked together and because Plato overlooks the significant biological differences between men and women.[24] Now, it should be pointed out that Plato anticipates and responds to these two objections. The sight of naked women exercising may be ridiculous "as things stand now," but with changes in practice attitudes will change also. As Plato notes, it was not long ago that the sight of men exercising naked was considered ridiculous. To Plato, only what is harmful or base is truly ridiculous (*Rep.* 452a–e). Bloom fastens on the fact that Plato minimizes the difference between women and men, which Plato compares to the difference between baldness and long-hairedness, a comparison he views as ridiculous.[25]

Bloom's argument does not hold up. He simply ignores Plato's express warning not to ignore important distinctions (454a–b). To Plato, just as the difference between baldness and long-hairedness has little bearing on one's ability to function as a carpenter, so being female or male has little bearing on one's ability to function as a ruler. Differences in people's natures are relevant only insofar as they bear on their qualifications to follow particular pursuits.

The community of the family is perhaps more vulnerable to criticism. Bloom contends that it places impossibly heavy burdens on the inhabitants of the just city. The Guardians renounce not only property but their families as well, and the possibility of ever knowing the identity of their children. However, Plato's response, again, is based on the power of education. He believes that people's emotional energy can be channeled; the concern they presently focus on property and family can be redirected into a powerful attachment to the city as a whole—which is of course his main reason for proposing this set of institutions in the first place. Bloom simply denies Plato's basic premise. He contends that these urges are ineradicable. Because they are associated with each person's self, with his body, Bloom argues that in overlooking them Plato "forgets the body."[26] But again, this argument has little weight unless it could be shown that Plato did not actually believe in the plasticity of human nature and the power of education, which Bloom has not shown.[27]

Aside from these problems with Bloom's arguments, I believe an additional consideration shows that Plato is quite serious about his treatment of women and the family. The point to note is that Plato limits the applicability of his proposals to the Guardians. The lowest class is to retain some semblance of the traditional family, while the reason for this is, presumably, that their inferior natures could not tolerate the demands that community of the family would impose on them. Along similar lines, Plato takes into account the fact that sexual deprivation must give rise to hostility even among the Guardians. This is the reason for the rigged lottery system he institutes, to lead frustrated Guardians to focus their hostility on chance instead of their rulers (*Rep.* 459c–60a). Surely, if Plato had wished to create a system of institutions that could not possibly work, he would have created it for the entire population of the city—as

Aristophanes did in *Ecclesiazusae*—and not confined it to those individuals he believed to be naturally suited.[28]

An additional set of reasons supports the claim that Plato is serious about implementing the just city. Evidence external to the dialogues is, I believe, unequivocal.

Let us return to the *Seventh Epistle*. If we accept this as genuine, it provides powerful evidence of Plato's seriousness of purpose. After recounting his early political experiences, Plato reports that these led him to believe "that the ills of the human race would never end until those who are sincerely and truly lovers of wisdom come into political power, or the rulers of our cities, by the grace of God, learn true philosophy" (326a–b). Immediately following this statement, Plato writes: "Such was the conviction I had when I arrived in Italy and Sicily for the first time" (326b). Scholars generally date Plato's first voyage to Sicily in 387. The *Republic* is generally said to have been written in the mid-370s.[29] Accordingly, not only does Plato declare his adherence to the idea of the philosopher-king, but he indicates that he had been thinking about the idea for some ten to fifteen years before constructing his greatest political dialogue on its basis. This evidence is flatly inconsistent with claims to the effect that the philosopher-king is introduced in the *Republic* to call attention to the impossibility of wholesale political reform. In order for Strauss and Bloom—and other scholars—to maintain that Plato's idea of the philosopher-king is not intended to be taken seriously, they must either explain away Plato's commitment to the philosopher-king in the *Seventh Epistle* or demonstrate that the epistle is not genuine. To the best of my knowledge, neither of these possibilities has been realized.[30]

There is additional evidence. Not only did Plato travel to Sicily two times with the intention of combining political power and philosophic wisdom in the person of Dionysius II, but he established the Academy as, at least in part, a training school for lawgivers and advisers of rulers.[31] Glenn Morrow, a leading scholar of Plato's later political theory, connects the Academy's political environment with Plato's observation in the *Epistle* that it is impossible to effect political improvements "without friends and loyal followers" (325c–d). He notes that it would have been unusual for the Academy not to have had political purposes, as all other similar associations that had been founded previously were "more or less political in character."[32]

There is evidence that several of Plato's students and associates took part in political reforms. Plutarch reports that Phormio drew up legislation for Elis, Eudoxus for Cnidus, and Aristotle for the Stagirites. Aristonymus was sent to Arcadia and Menedemus to the Pyrrhaens, while Alexander the Great is reported to have requested advice concerning kingship from Xenocrates, who was third head of the Academy (Plutarch, *Adv. Colot.* xxxii). According to Diogenes Laertius—who, however, is frequently unreliable—Plato himself was asked by the Thebans to draw up laws for the city of Megalopolis, which they founded (D. L., III, 23). Other sources report that two additional members of the Academy, Erastus and Corsicus, were sent to advise Hermeias, tyrant of Atarneus. The *Sixth Epistle,* probably spurious, concerns their mission. In addition, Aristotle was of course tutor to Alexander the Great, while Dion was a close associate of Plato. Several members of the Academy accompanied Dion on his expedition, including Callipus, who later assassinated him.[33] As we can see from this list, the Academy was involved in political activities of two kinds—drawing up the laws for new cities or attempting to advise rulers how to rule more wisely and justly. The extent to which any of these episodes was intended to realize the full-blown political theory of the *Republic* cannot be determined. As with Syracuse, it is unlikely that Plato or his associates attempted anything so grandiose. A likely hypothesis is that these reformers attempted to move cities as far along the path to virtue and harmony as was possible under the circumstances.

It must be borne in mind that the efforts of the Academy did not exist in a vacuum. As Morrow's observation concerning the political intentions of previous schools indicates, there was a long tradition in Greece of political involvement by philosophical schools. Most notable were the Pythagoreans,[34] a school with which Plato had close philosophical affinities.[35] In the *Seventh Epistle,* Plato notes his friendship with Archytas of Tarentum (338c), who is the addressee of the probably spurious *Ninth* and *Twelfth Epistles.* Archytas was a Pythagorean philosopher-politician, seven times general of his city, and said never to have been defeated in battle.[36] Even more interesting was Epaminondas, the leading figure in

Thebes and probably the most prominent person in the Greek world in the twenty or so years before his death, in 361, the period during which Plato was writing the *Republic*. As noted above, Epaminondas was a student of the Pythagorean philosopher, Lysis. He also lived in accordance with Pythagorean precepts. Although he was not a philosopher-king in the full sense, Aristotle remarks in the *Rhetoric* in reference to him: "At Thebes, as soon as those who had the conduct of affairs became philosophers, the city flourished" (*Rhet.* 1398b18).[37]

We have little evidence about Archytas or Epaminondas—or perhaps other figures who might have attracted Plato's attention—although there is little reason to believe that either attempted fundamental moral reform, let alone anything as grandiose as the *Republic*. Moreover, it is important to note that both of these figures attained political power through election, which would have limited their capacity to enact large-scale reforms, had they wished to. But in spite of these limitations, the overall accumulation of evidence presented here should render less implausible the claim that Plato was interested in combining philosophy and political power in the interest of substantial political reform.

CHAPTER FOUR

Three Theorists of Reform: More, Machiavelli, and Rousseau

Variations on the themes we have seen are found in subsequent writers. I focus on three examples, Thomas More, Machiavelli, and Rousseau, all of whom confronted the question of power in relation to their desired reforms. More explores the possibility of converting a reigning monarch. Machiavelli presents a timeless analysis of the costs and benefits of seizing power. Rousseau is a more complicated case. Influenced by the pioneering social science of Montesquieu, he moves beyond the belief that power alone is enough and presents a clearly reasoned account of the preconditions of moral reform. But in regard to the question of power, he has little to offer, falling back in the *Social Contract* on the great soul of an imagined, individual lawgiver. In his own life, Rousseau confronted the possibility of reforming actual states on two occasions, in regard to Corsica and Poland. Comparing his reactions to the two cases, we will see that while he apparently wished to follow something like the *Social Contract* blueprint in regard to Corsica, for Poland he took adverse circumstances into account and was surprisingly moderate.

MORE'S UTOPIAN VISION

More's *Utopia* is probably the most celebrated work in the utopian tradition, the work that of course gave the tradition its name. There is something timelessly appealing about the egalitarian, communistic, ideal society that More sketches, based on common sense and leavened with his famous wit. The main features and institutions of Utopia are too well known to require much summary. The centerpiece is the economic system. As in a monastery, which in large part provided More's model, everyone is required to work, though only six hours a day. The working day can be cut back because of the large number of idlers in existing European societies — lords, hangers on, monks, and so on — all of whom must work, and the anticonsumerist ethos of the society. All Utopians dress alike. Clothing is sturdy and simple, made to last two years. Home furnishings are similar, and people do not become overly attached to their homes, because these are redistributed by lot every ten years. Meals are in common, in public dining halls. Utopians are allowed to eat at home but prefer not to, as this takes far more work and the food is less good. Most famous, gold and silver are deglamorized, used for chamber pots and chains on slaves. The intention is to stop people from thinking about property and accumulating more than their neighbors. Provided with what they need and secure in their expectations for the future, the Utopians turn their leisure time to culture and education.

The society combines elements of the open and the quasi-totalitarian. Religion is remarkably tolerant for the time the work was written. People are allowed to worship as they please, with stern penalties for reviling the religions of others. Permissible beliefs are restricted, however, in that all utopians must believe that the soul does not die with the body and that the universe is divinely governed. But even those who do not hold these views are not punished, though they are subject to general opprobrium and not allowed to hold public offices. The aim of life in Utopia is enjoyment, for the Utopians hold that human happiness consists mainly of pleasure. This is as God intended, for people naturally pursue pleasure. But success here requires recognizing true pleasures and renouncing illusory enjoyments such as thinking oneself better than others because one has more expensive clothes.

This open and tolerant side of Utopia is combined with conformity enforced by public scrutiny. Work is unavoidable: "Everyone has his eye on you, so you're practically forced to get on with your job, and make some proper use of your spare time."[1] In church children sit in front of their parents, so "everyone's conduct in public is watched by those who are responsible for his discipline at home" (p. 126). In the main it is the constant pressure of public opinion that ensures adherence to societal norms and the smooth running of society.

More's reliance on public opinion is of a piece with his moral views in *Utopia*. In spite of its idealized quality, the ideal state inhabits a world that is not ideal. More provides lengthy accounts of how the Utopians wage war. There is also crime, including sexual transgressions, punished by slavery. On the whole the work makes greater concessions to the existing order of things than do many other utopian compositions. The state is not based on the heroic virtue of Spartan warriors or the complete self-abnegation of Plato's Guardians. More devotes relatively little attention to education. He does not take things to the Platonic extreme of using all the resources of the state to combat human nature. Rather, as is seen in his discussion of pleasure, Utopia allows human inclinations to follow their natural bent, though turned aside from harmful and illusory pleasures. The resulting social system is more sensible (according to general opinion) though less ingenious than what Plato propounds. Perhaps it is the more practical nature of his construction that More refers to in the poem by Utopia's poet laureate that he includes at the beginning of the work: "Plato's *Republic* now I claim / To match, or beat at its own game" (p. 27). As this specimen of Utopian poetry proclaims, Utopia is a land "without philosophy" (p. 27).

More identifies the great foe of human happiness as pride. In Utopia enforced equality and the absence of material means of differentiation put pride in its place, thereby eliminating "the root-causes of ambition, political conflict, and everything like that" (*Utopia,* p. 131). Pointedly, More observes that pride "is too deeply ingrained in human nature to be easily eradicated" (p. 131). The Utopians, rather, arrange moral institutions to control it and so are able to avoid the horrors it wreaks on the rest of mankind. I quote J. C. Davis:

> Utopia is a holding operation, a set of strategies to maintain social order and perfection in the face of the deficiencies, not to say hostility, of nature and the wilfulness of men.[2]

As the Manuels put this: "[More's] Utopian is not a 'new man' in the Abbot Joachim's or Thomas Müntzer's sense. He is a modified 'old man,' not wholly good by nature but capable of both good and evil, and the best in him is elicited by appropriate institutional arrangements."[3]

In spite of the work's place at the pinnacle of the utopian tradition, aspects of *Utopia* are intended to suggest practical reforms. The clearest instance concerns penal reform. Instead of executing thieves, More suggests that they be set to work in a form of slavery. In Book I the main spokesperson, Raphael Hythloday, bemoans the barbarity of current legal practice in England. Enclosure has thrown people off their land, leaving them to starve, beg, or steal. The last course is harshly repressed, as Raphael reports seeing as many as twenty thieves hanged on a single gallows. To provide a preferable alternative means of dealing with thieves, he describes the practice of penal servitude in the land of Tallstoria—which is similar to the system in Utopia (pp. 104–5)— and calls for its adoption in England. The King could begin by postponing a few death sentences, to see how the alternative system would work (pp. 53–54).

More realizes, however, that things will not change fundamentally until property is abolished. He refers to Plato's view, in Book IV of the *Republic*, that complex legal codes are futile (see above, p. 50). As with the treatment of chronic invalids, laws address only symptoms; they do not get to the root of the matter and attempt a cure: "But there's no hope of a cure, as long as private property continues" (*Utopia*, p. 66). *Utopia* is undoubtedly written in large part to call attention to this contention, presented in the form of a fable.

In spite of its standing as the archetypal utopian work, *Utopia* also departs from the strictures of the pure utopia in raising the question of political power. This is a major theme in Book I of the work, in the so-called dialogue of counsel. The discussion here is structurally distinct from the bulk of the work, which is devoted to the ideal society. It was also written separately. As J. H. Hexter has shown, this section of Book I was a later addition to the work, perhaps to dramatize an internal struggle More experienced when he was beginning his career in the court of Henry VIII.[4] Thus this section of the work is far more political than what is found in pure utopias. The dialogue of counsel, like the work as a whole, is a dramatized conversation between Raphael and More himself (the "More-character"), with occasional participation by Peter Gilles, an actual friend of More's and Erasmus's. The dialogue form allows More to distance himself from the radical ideas his work advances, by putting them into the mouth of Raphael and reserving far more conventional, pragmatic opinions for himself.

The dialogue of counsel begins with Peter asking Raphael why he does not enter government service. The latter responds with a grim assessment of the possibility of meaningful accomplishments from such a position. The More-character cites Plato's teaching on the need to combine philosophy and kingship. Raphael replies that Plato believed that it was necessary for kings to be philosophers. Otherwise they would never listen to philosophers, as "kings are too deeply infected with wrong ideas in childhood to take any philosopher's advice" (*Utopia*, p. 57). This lesson, Raphael notes, Plato himself learned by experience with Dionysius (*Utopia*, p. 57). Under present conditions, it is useless to propose policies that contravene existing practices. For instance, in the court of the King of France, when the Cabinet is planning territorial expansion, in Italy, what would happen if Hythloday proposed a complete reversal of policy? It is clear that this advice would be ignored (pp. 57–59). The nature of a royal court also renders success a remote possibility. Courtiers are vain and pompous; they respond to any new suggestion as an affront to their reputations. They think they will look foolish unless they can find objections to whatever is proposed. Raphael describes their "curious mixture of conceit, stupidity, and stubbornness" (p. 43). Courtiers are also sycophants, adjusting their opinions to those of their ruler, changing course on a dime to keep pace with his (pp. 55–56). Under such conditions, the More-character agrees, to propose reforms is futile:

What possible good could it do? How can [courtiers] be expected to take in a totally unfamiliar line of thought, which goes against all their deepest prejudices? That sort of thing is quite fun in a friendly conversation, but at a Cabinet meeting, where major decisions of policy have to be made, such philosophizing would be completely out of place.

Raphael's response: "there's no room at Court for philosophy" (p. 63).

The More-character notes that the philosopher at court can make a contribution. Though he cannot hope to put across entirely new ideas, he can act to improve things, to do as much good and as little harm as possible (p. 64). It does not require imaginative reach to suppose that More himself had some such intention in deciding to serve Henry VIII. But what can be expected through this means falls far short of radical change. As noted above, in his account of Utopian society, More indicates the futility of attempting significant improvements through piecemeal reforms, which address only symptoms, without getting to the root of society's problems.

Thus More is well aware of the need for political power but sees the impediments to attaining it. Because *Utopia* confines attention to the possibility of gaining influence over a sitting ruler and never broaches the question of seizing power, More is somewhat like Plato in seeing the great potential of combining wisdom and power but does not know how to achieve this. Thus it is notable that the ideal society in the work is represented as the result of such a combination. Utopia was founded by King Utopus. Little is said of Utopus, aside from the fact that he conquered the territory and converted it from a peninsula into an island by excavating a channel, cutting it off from the mainland (pp. 69–70). Utopus is also said to have designed the layout for the island's fifty-four towns—and presumably the overall layout of the island as well (p. 73). Obviously a tolerant spirit, he is also responsible for the society's religious regulations (p. 119). Beyond this, Utopus is a shadowy figure. But the futility expressed in the dialogue of counsel, in Book I, stands alongside the embodiment of a figure who combined both power and wisdom and so was able to found an ideal society.

In *Utopia* nothing more is said about the process through which the society was begun. In comparison to other ideal societies, Utopia requires relatively little of people and so would be relatively easy to establish. Because Utopia takes men much as they are and channels their energies, the problems of designing an intensive educational system and, accompanying this, the problem of the first generation would be less severe than with other utopian works. Of course, the force of habit in the existing generation could not be allowed to subvert the system during the time it is taking hold. But again, as More requires less of people than does Plato, measures such as cleaning the canvas of the state, expelling everyone over the age of ten, need not be discussed. But even if Utopia is a limited ideal in these important ways, it cannot get off the ground unless it is supported by political authority, which remains an insuperable obstacle.

MACHIAVELLI AND RADICAL POLITICAL REFORM

While More examines the problems encountered on one prong of Plato's fork, Machiavelli explores the other. Machiavelli was not a systematic thinker. His greatness lay in precise observation. Because he studied a range of historical cases, he provides valuable lessons on many important political topics, including radical reform. In the *Prince* he is concerned mainly with how to retain power and pays relatively little attention to what power is to be used for. But a major subject of the *Discourses* is the reform of corrupted states. Machiavelli generally focuses on relatively small political entities, mainly Rome and other ancient cities and the Italian city-states of his own day. Rife with political instability, palace coups, and revolutions, these states provided opportunities for founding what Machiavelli viewed as ideal societies. Picking through his diverse discussions, we can extract his main lessons in this area.

There are inherent problems in using Machiavelli's works. He can be criticized for being remarkably credulous about historical sources and also for lacking historical sense. He did not consider differences between ancient and Renaissance political affairs.[5] To some extent he was able to do this because he focused narrowly on political rule, with considerably less attention to the context in which rule is exercised. His political teachings were also decisively affected by his cyclical view of history and conception of human nature as unchanging.

> He who considers present affairs and ancient ones readily understands that all cities and all peoples have the same desires and the same traits and that they always have had them. He who diligently examines past events easily foresees future ones in every country and can apply to them the remedies used by the ancients, or, not finding any that have been used, can devise new ones because of the similarity of the events. (*Dis.*, I, 39, p. 278)[6]

In reading the *Discourses*, one is tempted to dismiss the cyclical account of history, taken over from the Greek historian Polybius (*Dis.*, I, 2). But it clearly was central to Machiavelli's thought, as is seen in his continual discussion of states' rise and fall and in his view concerning unchanging human nature.

It is because of his opinion of what unchanging human nature is like that Machiavelli provides a valuable account of the political realities of radical reform. For the would-be lawgiver, the reality of human nature constitutes a severe impediment.

> As it is demonstrated by all those who discuss life in a well-ordered state—and history is full of examples—it is necessary for him who lays out a state and arranges laws for it to presuppose that all men are evil and that they are always going to act according to the wickedness of their spirits whenever they have free scope; and when any wickedness remains hidden for a time, the reason is some hidden cause which, in the lack of any experience of the contrary, is not recognized, but then its discovery is brought about by Time, which they say is the father of every Truth. (*Dis.*, I, 3, p. 201)

When the proclivities of human nature become manifest, they have to be dealt with.

In spite of his interest in reform, Machiavelli devotes relatively little attention to processes through which human nature can be recast. Like

Plutarch, he plumbs the history of Sparta as a moral exemplar, but unlike Plutarch, he does not provide in-depth analysis of the educational system on which Spartan virtue was grounded. The *agōgē* is rarely if ever mentioned in the *Prince* or *Discourses,* although the Spartan constitution is discussed, especially in reference to how its balance of institutions allowed it to counteract forces of decline lodged in history's cycles (*Dis.,* I, 2). Machiavelli also discusses details of Spartan history, especially the attempted reforms of Agis and Cleomenes, during Hellenistic times. Perhaps it was because Rome achieved the pinnacle of virtue without state-run education[7] that Machiavelli is not much concerned with this subject. He focuses, rather, on the mechanics of power, as if believing that if these are controlled other desiderata will follow. To the extent that he discusses the preconditions for the founding of a new state, Machiavelli generally considers the conditions necessary for attaining political power. As J. W. Allen says of Machiavelli: "He saw very clearly, but he did not see very much."[8] But as a theorist of power, Machiavelli's reputation is deserved. It is because he recognized the central role of power in political reform that he observed: "[T]here is nothing more difficult to plan or more uncertain of success or more dangerous to carry out than an attempt to introduce new institutions" (*Pr.,* chap. 6, p. 26)

We find in Machiavelli's writings a set of rules or lessons that the would-be reformer must observe. Most central and perhaps best known is a precept apparently formulated on observing Savonarola in his native Florence. Reform requires power; unarmed prophets go to the gallows. In Machiavelli's words: "This is the reason why all armed prophets win, and unarmed ones fall" (*Pr.,* chap. 6, p. 26) People's characters are variable. It is easier to persuade them initially than to keep them persuaded. When they no longer believe, it is necessary to be able to compel continued belief. After Savonarola had instituted his new order, when the multitude began to lose faith in him, he had no means to maintain belief (p. 22). Machiavelli takes things one step farther. Not only must the reformer have recourse to force, but he must concentrate all power in himself. This lesson is drawn from the story of Romulus and Remus; the former's fratricide is justified on this ground (*Dis.,* I, 9).

If concentration of power is necessary for the reformer, the question becomes how this is attained. Machiavelli does not address this directly, but he draws sobering lessons of power politics. Most important, if successful reform requires that all power be in the new lawgiver's hands, then the state's future depends entirely on his good intentions—to say nothing of additional requirements concerning his ability to use his power effectively. The problem here is compounded by the means necessary to attain power.

> To reorganize a city for living under good government assumes a good man; therefore a good man will seldom attempt to become prince by evil methods, even though his purposes be good; on the other hand a wicked man, when he has become prince, will seldom try to do what is right, for it never will come into his mind to use rightly the authority he has gained wickedly. (*Dis.*, I, 18, p. 243)

Machiavelli does not systematically examine attainment of power. He has little faith in the possibility of gaining influence over a prince through persuasion. In fact, one precept in the *Prince* is that rulers should not take unsolicited advice (chap. 23), although, dedicated to Lorenzo de Medici, the *Prince* is precisely that. It is toward the other alternative that Machiavelli gravitates and which he analyzes in detail.

The lengthiest chapter of the *Discourses,* Book III, chapter 6, examines conspiracies. Although Machiavelli says that this was written to help princes "learn how to guard themselves against these dangers" (p. 428), from another point of view, the chapter provides a handbook for conspirators. Most examples concern conspiracies against monarchs or tyrants. Machiavelli cites only a few examples bearing on republics.

The chapter is a somber account. The impediments to success are recounted in detail, supported with numerous examples. Conspirators confront perils at all stages, in the planning, the execution, and the aftermath of their action. In the first stage, the dangers of betrayal are so great that only few highly trusted confederates can be confided in, a precept Machiavelli supports, once again, with abundant examples. The difficulties of execution are recounted in similar detail, with attention to the vagaries of chance that can upset even the most careful plans. Machiavelli believes that, in general, the only realistic conspiracies involve persons close to the prince, who have access to his person. Fellow conspirators must be not only faithful and trustworthy but also experienced in such things and so will not commit grievous errors under pressure. Perhaps the main lesson, as in much of Machiavelli's political thought, is the importance of boldness and resolution, striking at the first opportunity rather than waiting for ideal circumstances.

In assessing Machiavelli's lessons, it is necessary to bear in mind that most of his conspiracies amount to little more than political assassination, with the conspirators believing that when the blow was struck power would be theirs for the taking. Of course, the problems of seizing power increase exponentially when we move beyond one-person rule and more so when we consider larger, more populous territories. Machiavelli notes that seizing power in a popular state is possible only when the people have become corrupt (*Dis.,* III, 8). But there is a great distance between his examples and politics beyond the city-state.

Exactly what the ruler is to do with his power is not examined systematically. Machiavelli of course presents valuable precepts on ruling, especially in regard to maintaining power. But aside from the importance of religion, he provides relatively little guidance about how the new order of things is to be established. His advice to rulers includes above all the need to eliminate all members of the previous ruling family and to do what it takes to stymie opposition. It follows from Machiavelli's unsentimental view of politics that whoever enters the political arena should be prepared to do what is necessary to achieve his goals, although, as Machiavelli timelessly argues, doing so is often incompatible with being good. A classic expression of this aspect of the dilemma of political reform is Machiavelli's account of the extraordinary measures taken by Philip of Macedon. Philip reorganized the government of his country, destroying old cities and building new ones, moving populations from place to place, and otherwise leaving nothing unchanged. Machiavelli writes:

> These methods are very cruel, and enemies to all government not merely Christian but human, and any man ought to avoid them and prefer to live a private life rather than to be a king who brings such ruin on men. Notwithstanding, a ruler who does not wish to take that

first good way of lawful government, if he wishes to maintain himself, must enter upon this evil one. (*Dis.*, I, 26, p. 254)

Machiavelli does not pull his punches in describing the necessary steps as evil. But although they are evil according to the standards of traditional (Judeo-Christian) morality, they are necessary nevertheless. To shrink from them is to court failure. But because they entail so much suffering, many rulers do shrink. Such rulers desire political ends but are not willing to employ the necessary means. They pursue "certain middle ways," as Machiavelli calls them, which are "very injurious" (p. 254).

Machiavelli pursues the implications of his political views with a ruthless logicality akin to that of Plato. Many people who have written on politics have been blinded by wishful sentimentality. The *Discourses,* like the *Prince,* was intended to be "something useful" (*Pr.,* chap. 15, p. 57). A ruler who wishes to be good (in the traditional sense) "will surely be destroyed among so many who are not good" (ibid.). Machiavelli pursues this insight to its unsettling conclusion. A good state will be a rarity, requiring a fortunate confluence of events. But while Plato draws back from political violence without in-depth discussion, Machiavelli provides the details. The politics of moral reform is an extension of ordinary politics, beset with the same obstacles and frightening moral dilemmas. Reform is necessary because people are not good. But because they are not good, the reformer must be concerned with the exigencies of power politics, which are not good either.

A great advantage of reform through persuasion is that it avoids the moral paradoxes Machiavelli lays out. But it is able to do so only by casting aside any realistic chance of success. The would-be reformer must be armed, with all this implies.

Both the *Prince* and the *Discourses* present examples of successful lawgivers and reformers. These include Moses, Cyrus, Romulus, and Theseus (*Pr.,* chap. 6), all, one will note, legendary (or quasi-legendary) figures. The same could be said of Lycurgus, another of Machiavelli's examples.[9] The dimension of the difficulties in bringing about successful reform is indicated by the fact that Machiavelli's chief examples, whom he advises his readers to emulate, are figures from mythology.

Rousseau and Political Reform

The themes I have traced through More and Machiavelli are also prominent in the work of Rousseau. One can question the extent to which
Rousseau was interested in realizing the ideal state described in the *Social Contract*. For instance, according to Judith Shklar, Rousseau was "a
social critic, the most devastating of them all, and not a designer of plans
for political reform."[10] But like More and Machiavelli, he confronted the
political impediments to radical reform. Although he probably never
imagined that his ideal society could be brought into existence, this was
because of political impediments that he recognized. Like Plato and
More, he turned away from violent realization of his plans. But he did
not turn toward converting a person in authority. Rather, like Plato, he
put whatever faith he had in a miraculous occurrence, the lawgiver of the
Social Contract. However, in spite of the dim prospects for Rousseau's
utopia, on at least two occasions he was asked to draw up constitutions
for existing states and so considered having his ideals realized in this
fashion. While his unfinished *Constitutional Project for Corsica* is in
many ways consistent with the political principles advanced in the *Social
Contract*, his *Considerations on the Government of Poland* departs sharply.
To consider Rousseau as a theorist of radical reform, we will examine his
recommendations for Corsica and Poland, before returning to his most
sustained discussion of the topic, in Book II, chapter 7, of the *Social
Contract*.

In one sense Rousseau's ideas on radical reform are more sophisticated than any I have considered to this point. In addition to thinking about
the means through which his ideal state could be realized, Rousseau systematically considered the necessary conditions a society must have to be
capable of reform. This is probably because of the influence of Montesquieu's pioneering inquiries into social science. In *Emile* Rousseau comments on Montesquieu's contribution to the "vast and useless" science of
politics. Instead of concerning himself with "the principles of political
right; he was content to deal with the positive laws of settled governments; and nothing could be more different than these two branches of
study."[11] But in spite of Rousseau's preference for pondering what ought

to be rather than what is, his own political theorizing was heavily influenced by his great predecessor. Intimations of preconditions are seen in Machiavelli. For example, Machiavelli notes that in order to be suitable for a republic, a state's citizens must be relatively equal economically; if they are unequal, they are better suited for a monarchy.[12] But as with many subjects, Machiavelli touches on this only in passing.

Rousseau approaches matters more systematically. His ideal state is a republic, generally similar to Sparta and Rome — and to the republic as discussed in Montesquieu's *Spirit of the Laws.* Like Montesquieu, Rousseau does not believe all forms of government are suited to all countries. A government must be in accord with a country and its people's character. One should give a people the best institutions possible for their particular circumstances, though these may not be the best in an absolute sense (*S.C.,* Bk. II, chap. 11, p. 171). Rousseau realizes that his preferred form of government is not possible everywhere: "Since liberty is not a fruit of every climate, it is not within the reach of all peoples" (Bk. III, chap. 8, p. 187).

The people to be reformed must be fresh and vigorous, unspoiled by established laws and customs: "Liberty can be acquired, but it can never be recovered" (p. 166). To be suitable for a republic, a given territory must be small. Its resources must be sufficient to support the population but not a great deal more than that. There must be strong ties of common interest among the people (Bk. II, chap. 10, p. 169) and little economic inequality. Although property need not be equal, "no citizen should be so rich as to be capable of buying another citizen, and none so poor that he is forced to sell himself" (chap. 11, p. 170). The state must also enjoy a period of peace while the new laws take effect. Rousseau recognizes that a territory meeting all his conditions will be difficult to find. The only country in Europe capable of receiving proper laws is Corsica (Bk. II, chap. 10, p. 170).

It is interesting but not coincidental that in 1764 Rousseau was asked "to trace the plan of a political system" for Corsica. At that time the island was in the midst of a protracted struggle for independence from the Republic of Genoa. Attracted by Rousseau's favorable mention in the *Social Contract,* Corsican officers turned to Rousseau, "the wise man capable of providing the means to preserve that freedom which it has cost so much blood to win."[13] Rousseau was thrilled at the invitation: "[T]he very idea lifts my soul and transports me," he wrote.[14] Rousseau agreed, but his *Constitutional Project for Corsica* was left incomplete, as political exigencies eliminated the possibility of reform. The work is very much a rough draft, not only unfinished, but possibly never reread by the author.[15] But in spite of its condition, the piece is important for what it tells us about Rousseau's ideas concerning political reform under circumstances he viewed as ideal. His thoughts on Corsica are especially interesting if considered in the light of his views on reform in Poland, which also approached him for constitutional advice. Thus I will also examine the *Considerations on the Government of Poland*, which was Rousseau's last political work.

In the *Constitutional Project for Corsica*, Rousseau notes again that no people is more suited for good government than the Corsicans. In designing its institutions, he had a fairly free hand, going so far as to envision inaugurating the state with a formal oath, the terms of which are in accord with the contractual formula in the *Social Contract:*

> In the name of God Almighty, and on the holy Gospels, by a sacred and irrevocable oath, I join myself—body, goods, will and all my powers—to the Corsican nation; granting to her the full ownership of me—myself and all that depends upon me. I swear to live and die for her, to observe all her laws, and to obey her lawful Chiefs and Magistrates in all things conformable to the Law. So may God be my help in this life, and have mercy on my soul.[16]

One will note that the degree of surrender expressed here is irrevocable and complete, as in the *Social Contract*.

In preparing for the work, Rousseau requested as much information as possible about the island, about its commercial and social conditions, history, geography, politics, and so on, and "everything that serve[d] to reveal the national character."[17] Healthy and vigorous, the Corsicans are well suited for a new system. Although they are without the vices of other nations, they are infected with undesirable prejudices, the elimination of which is central to the new republic (*Corsica*, p. 278). As Maurice Cranston notes, Rousseau's work is not a constitution in the usual sense of the term but rather an outline of political, economic, and social elements of civil associations.[18] Rousseau's basic model is the ancient republic, a state based on subsistence agriculture with a republican government, affording the people high degrees of participation and hence equality. "This is the fundamental principle of our new constitution" (*Corsica*, p. 286).

As in the *Social Contract* and other political works, Rousseau aims to combine equality of citizenship with approximate economic equality. His proposals in this direction occupy the bulk of the extant text. As in the *Social Contract*, he does not preach socialism but promotes equality through highly circumscribed private property: "[M]y idea . . . is not to destroy private property absolutely, since that is impossible, but to confine it within the narrowest possible limits, to give it a measure, a rule, a rein which will contain, direct, and subjugate it, and keep it ever subordinate to the public good" (p. 317). Along similar lines, Rousseau wishes sharply to curtail commerce. There is to be no foreign trade and as little internal trade as possible; each farmer is to satisfy his needs from his own land. Although there is to be gradation of classes based on ownership of land, the agricultural economy is to allow little economic inequality: "Everyone should make a living, and no one should grow rich; that is the fundamental principle of the prosperity of the nation" (p. 308). Rousseau realizes that this is not a path to wealth, but this does not concern him: "It is better for the land to produce a little less and for the inhabitants to lead better regulated lives" (p. 309). The government should be funded through a public domain, with citizens providing their labor on *corvées* for public works. Through these reforms, the influence of money is to be reduced as much as possible.

Unfortunately, the work breaks off and Rousseau covers few additional topics. But from what we have seen, it is clear that he concentrates on reforming the moral substance of the polity. To recapture the virtue of ancient peoples, one must replicate their hardy rustic way of life. Rousseau notes that his proposals will need emendation as time goes on (p. 285). Presumably, virtuous citizens will be able to move farther along in the direction of virtue. But the state's overall course should remain in pursuit of rustic equality.

Considerations on the Government of Poland is sharply different. This work resulted from a request from the Polish government for advice about

proposed reforms, during a period of crisis. Rousseau set about study-
ing the complicated social and political history of Poland, devoting six
months to this task.[19] Given the less than ideal circumstances of Poland,
Rousseau's response was far more modest than his proposals for Corsica or what he envisions in the *Social Contract.* As Cranston notes, in
this work Rousseau expresses the conservative side of his political thinking.[20] Although he viewed Poland as a corrupt state, with many undesirable features, Rousseau believed it was necessary to preserve what
was good in the existing order: "Worthy Poles, beware! Beware lest, in
your eagerness to improve, you may worsen your constitution" (*Poland,*
chap. 1, p. 160). His attitude toward reform was cautious: "I do not say
that things must be left in their present state; but I do say that they must
be touched only with extreme circumspection" (chap. 1, p. 161).

At that time the Polish political system was an elective monarchy. The
bulk of the population was serfs, who were deprived of civil rights. Yet
Rousseau was willing to countenance the existing system of representative government as long as there were more frequent diets and representatives more closely followed the instructions of their constituents. He
did not propose to abolish the monarchy but only to make sure it was
actually elective. Even the condition of the serfs, whom he recognized as
being "less than nothing" (chap. 6, p. 183), should not be changed, until
they could be made fit to be free.

> To free the common people of Poland would be a great and worthy
> enterprise, but bold, perilous, and not to be attempted lightly. Among
> the precautions to be taken, there is one which is indispensable and
> requires time; it is, before everything else, to make the serfs who are to
> be free worthy of liberty and capable of enduring it. (Chap. 6, p. 186)

The subject to which Rousseau devotes greatest attention is the development of moral character. Of education, he says: "This is the important question. It is education that must give souls a national formation,
and direct their opinions and tastes in such a way that they will be patriotic by inclination, by passion, by necessity" (chap. 4, p. 176). Thus he
focuses on public education, recommending public ceremonies for the
conferral of honors and other devices through which patriotic feelings

can be inculcated. Children's games should be conducted under the public eye. Great attention should be paid to signs of distinction through which honored citizens can be identified. Rousseau's overall approach is clear in the following passage.

> Work, therefore, without pause or relaxation, to bring patriotism to the highest pitch in every Polish heart. . . . [A]rrange things so that every citizen will feel himself to be constantly under the public eye; that no one will advance or succeed save by the favor of the public; that no office or position shall be filled save by the will of the nation; and finally that, from the lowliest nobleman, even from the lowliest peasant, up to the king, if possible, all shall be so dependent on public esteem that nothing can be done, nothing acquired, no success obtained without it. Out of the effervescence excited by this mutual emulation will arise that patriotic intoxication without which liberty is but an empty word, and laws but a chimera. (Chap. 11, p. 244)

In place of immediate, far-reaching reform, Rousseau hopes that measures such as these will affect the Poles' character, so as to make proper institutions more possible in the future.

Further details of Rousseau's proposals for Poland need not concern us. What interests us is what they reveal about his views concerning radical reform. It is well known that Rousseau's ideas in the *Social Contract* are radical. He views all existing societies as corrupt, crying for reform. His proposals for Poland reveal a different side. Given the impossibility of radical reform, he proposes more modest measures to improve existing conditions. As Montesquieu argues in *Spirit of the Laws,* Rousseau too believes that the reformer must recognize the complexity of political reality. Unless circumstances are as favorable as those of Corsica, he must proceed with care. He should attempt to improve conditions as much as possible, without risking making them worse. Even the corrupt institutions of Poland are recognized as better than possible alternatives.

In spite of his willingness to adapt proposed reforms to the conditions, Rousseau was not able actually to reform either country. Placed in the almost impossibly favorable position of being asked to make new laws for troubled states, he saw the invitations come to naught. His lack of success was in keeping with circumstances envisioned in the *Social Contract*, which recognizes the unlikelihood of successful reform. As we have seen with previous thinkers, the insurmountable problem was attaining a position with the requisite authority. The very fact that people require reform means they will probably resist it. This is a classic conundrum that Rousseau recognizes. In order for people willingly to accept proper laws, they must be virtuous. But the only way they can be in this condition, free from the corruption of existing societies, is if they have been brought up in a properly constituted state — which is not possible until good laws are accepted.

> For an emerging people to be capable of appreciating the sound maxims of politics and to follow the fundamental rules of statecraft, the effect would have to become the cause. The social spirit which ought to be the work of that institution, would have to preside over the institution itself. And men would be, prior to the advent of laws, what they ought to become by means of laws. (Bk. II, chap. 7, p. 164)

To solve this intractable problem, Rousseau introduces the idea of a supremely gifted lawgiver.

According to Rousseau, the lawgiver must remake men. Beginning with individuals, he must transform them into constituents of a societal whole. To succeed, he must know the passions of men but feel none of them. His happiness must be independent of the people's, but he must devote himself to their interests (pp. 162–63). In addition, he must pursue his aims without political power. Though the lawgiver is the central figure in establishing the state, he has no official role in it. Because of Rousseau's strict requirements of self-government, the lawgiver cannot make the laws. His proposals must be voted on and accepted by the people. His major task, then, is to persuade the people to accept his advice. Because the people are corrupt and self-interested, this will be no easy task: "Thus we find together in the work of legislation two things that seem incompatible: an undertaking that transcends human force, and, to execute it, an authority that is nil" (p. 164); "Gods would be needed to give men laws" (p. 163).

The only way Rousseau proposes to overcome these obstacles is the lawgiver's extraordinary personality. He must convince the people that he speaks with religious authority, that the gods are responsible for his wisdom. Though he can resort to devices such as oracles or stone tablets, it is his "great soul" that must carry conviction (pp. 164–65). If the people can be convinced to accept his laws, the state will be on its way.

Rousseau is able to support his faith in the lawgiver with historical examples. As one would expect, his favored instances are from ancient city-states, especially Sparta and Rome. In discussing the lawgiver in the *Social Contract,* he mentions Lycurgus (*S.C.,* Bk. II, chap. 7, p. 163). In the *Considerations on the Government of Poland,* he identifies three outstanding lawgivers: Lycurgus, Numa (of Rome), and Moses (chap. 2, p. 163). But in addition to ancient figures, in the *Social Contract* he also mentions Calvin as a lawgiver of genius (Bk. II, chap. 7, n. 7).

Like Machiavelli, then—to whom he refers directly (Bk. II, chap. 7, n. 8)—Rousseau's examples are primarily quasi-mythological figures. Aside from Calvin, the historical evidence for the achievements of Lycurgus, Numa, and Moses is not strong, and they are hardly models that an eighteenth-century politician could easily follow. Because Rousseau does not countenance violence as a means of reform, his hopes are left to rest on the intervention of miraculous forces. However, although "the great soul of the lawgiver" is not an adequate standard for revolutionaries to rally around, Rousseau's recognition of the preconditions of radical reform indicates that he would not support many actual movements for wholesale political change.

CHAPTER FIVE

The Jacobin Ideal

JACOBIN THEORY

Having surveyed highlights of the history of the political theory of radical reform, let us pause to assess what we have seen. An important point to note about the utopias discussed so far is that they are generally static. The societies are generally small and isolated. Once constructed, they are also intended to last, without substantial changes. These conditions are often clear in literary utopias; isolated from the world, they are out of touch with forces calling for development and change. Their timelessness contributes to their exotic appeal to the travelers who stumble upon them. Something of this timeless quality is seen in the utopias I have discussed. According to ancient tradition, Sparta maintained the institutions of Lycurgus for centuries. Though Plato does not say how long the ideal city in the *Republic* is intended to last—and recognizes the inevitability of its decline—he does note in the *Laws* that Magnesia should remain unchanged, like Egypt, for thousands of years (*Laws* 657a–b). As Popper notes, because Plato regards all change in his ideal societies as decline, the ability to remain static is built into their very structure.[1]

There is some recognition of change. Machiavelli distinguishes between static republics and republics built to expand

and notes necessary differences in their respective institutions. A society like Rome, built to expand, obviously cannot remain static, although the alternative society, such as Venice or Sparta, can remain unchanged for a protracted time.[2]

Scholars note that timelessness is generally characteristic of utopian societies before the industrial revolution. With change in the means of production occurring at a slow pace if at all, there is no need for ideal societies to evolve. Although timelessness contributes to the air of unreality of literary utopias, the theorists we have discussed are less unrealistic in other respects. This is perhaps most clear in their recognition of the need to deal with other societies. Sparta was of course built for war— though more to maintain control of captive, subject populations than for expansion. Plato recognizes the need to prepare for war in the *Republic* (422a–23b, 466e–71c), along lines followed closely by More in *Utopia*.[3] War is of course at the center of Machiavelli's republic for expansion, while the moral qualities developed in conflict are integral to the virtue that allows the state to prosper. But on the whole a governing motif in all these states is that once institutions are properly put in place, they do not change. Moral qualities developed by good laws in turn help the laws to function properly, and this virtuous circle can continue indefinitely.

Things change significantly with the Enlightenment and its accompanying idea of progress. Theorists begin to ground utopia in history, a future state to which we more closely approximate through time. The industrial revolution exacerbates this tendency. Technological development requires the ideal society to accommodate change, at least until nature has been mastered and human needs fulfilled with relative ease. In subsequent chapters I discuss these themes in regard to the Marxian tradition.

For our purposes, it is important to note that self-contained, static utopias allow for pure theories of implementation. This is most clear in Plato's *Republic*, in which the philosophers simply wipe the state clean and begin anew. Considerations apart from the initially corrupt society and its new rules need not be taken into account. Details are sketchier in regard to Lycurgus in Sparta, Rousseau's legislator in *The Social Contract*, or Utopus in his ideal society. I have noted Rousseau's attempts to come to terms with political realities in Poland and Corsica. But in these

other cases, outside factors do not significantly intervene. From the reformer's perspective, this of course is desirable, as it greatly simplifies matters. It also, however, limits the extent to which means of reform can be
applied to actual societies, especially if, as modern history has shown,
actual attempts at large-scale reform have occurred in the context of traumatic wars, cases in point being the French, Russian, and Chinese revolutions. History has shown that the social turmoil and widespread distress
that revolutions require are often products of war. As Theda Skocpol argues, when these factors are accompanied by a collapse of state authority,
thereby making revolution more possible, the conditions for radical change
are satisfied.[4]

The material I examine in the remainder of this book is concerned
with moving from the realm of pure theory to practice. I discuss Jacobinism in the French Revolution and the Marxian traditions—and its anarchist critics—moving into the Russian Revolution. In these cases the
simplicity of focus of Plato's philosopher-ruler or Lycurgus is brushed
aside by enormously complex social exigencies, including, in France and
Russia, the need to deal with a hostile outside world. However, I believe
the factors discussed in previous chapters are highly relevant in these circumstances. I will set aside many complex aspects of the two cases, focusing on attempts to realize utopia in theory and practice. The ideas discussed thus far will provide a kind of thread through the labyrinth in
large nation-states embroiled in conflict at home and in traumatic conflict
with other countries. In spite of dramatic differences in size and complexity of problems, there is strong continuity in regard to the funda-
ments of wholesale moral reform. In the *Republic* Plato says that analyz-
ing justice in the city is helpful for understanding justice in the soul; the
larger object can provide guidance for the smaller (*Rep.* 368c – 69a). For
our purposes, in the opposite direction, the problems encountered in
reforming smaller, more manageable societies can provide a road map of
sorts for larger, more complex cases.

If the theorists I have discussed are to help guide this further analysis, I should attempt to draw out their main lessons. A central conclusion
is the need for force. According to Machiavelli, unarmed prophets go to
the gallows. I have traced Plato's realization of the need for political power,
that philosophers must also be kings. According to Plutarch, Lycurgus

was backed by armed supporters, if only thirty men. King Utopus had an army behind him, while Rousseau's views support this precept in departing from it. In the absence of other means to persuade his recalcitrant targets, the lawgiver requires a miraculously great soul.

When we turn to modern nation-states, questions of force become far more serious. While Lycurgus was supported by a handful of men, in a country of millions armed supporters must number in the thousands or tens of thousands. If, as Machiavelli says, all power must be concentrated in the reformers' hands, the prospects of wholesale reform will depend heavily on their character and motivation. As we saw, Machiavelli's paradox centers on the difficulty of finding a man who is wicked enough to seize power but good enough to use it to reform his fellows. On a larger canvas, the severity of this problem increases exponentially. Rather than need a single virtuous individual, or a relative handful, a large society requires thousands of them. Where they are to come from is a question that must be addressed. If the society as a whole is corrupt, a virtuous remnant will obviously be more difficult to discover.

Central themes in the discussion to this point can be expressed in what I call a "Jacobin" theory of radical reform. Robespierre and the actual Jacobins are discussed in this chapter. There are six main items in a Jacobin theory. The guiding impetus is the desire to realize a set of ultimate values in society and the need for political power to accomplish this. The values take shape in a model for an ideal society, or, to use Popper's words, "a more or less clear and detailed description or blueprint" of an ideal society.[5]

I list the major components and then discuss them briefly.

(J.1) The plan or blueprint of the desired, ideal society;

(J.2) A low estimation of the potential of the vast majority of the inhabitants of existing society to conform to the dictates of (J.1) on their own;

(J.3) Belief in the existence of a small group of individuals who understand the blueprint and are strongly committed to its realization;

(J.4) Support of this group's, this minority's, seizure of political power;

(J.5) Use of the minority-controlled state to condition and reeducate the inhabitants of society in accordance with the dictates of (J.1);

(J.6) A distinctive theory of representation, which I will call "real representation."

As I use the concept, the logic of Jacobinism is rooted in (J.1) and (J.2).
The Jacobin believes in a plan for society, which, if implemented, would
eliminate the problems and abuses of society as it always has existed. The
problem, however, is that the vast majority of people are unable to grasp
the plan and so do not strive for its realization of their own accord. The
dilemma is clearly formulated by Rousseau in the *Social Contract,* in a
passage quoted above (p. 87):

> For an emerging people to be capable of appreciating the sound max-
> ims of politics and to follow the fundamental rules of statecraft, the
> effect would have to become the cause. The social spirit which ought
> to be the work of that institution, would have to preside over the in-
> stitution itself. And men would be, prior to the advent of laws, what
> they ought to become by means of laws. (Bk. II, chap. 7, p. 164)

The Jacobin not only believes that there is a solution to all social problems, but that society cannot be brought to embrace this without assistance. Distrusting the character of the mass of people, Jacobins argue
that the minority, who know the truth, must convey it to the majority.
Given their pessimism about the majority, expressed in (J.2), Jacobins
believe this can be done only if the minority has the resources of the state
at its disposal. Thus the minority must seize control of the state and use
it to educate the majority, to bring them to accept the one true plan. To use
the term introduced above, the Jacobin is an educational realist. He recognizes that intensive education is necessary to inculcate virtue. As we
saw in our discussion of Plato, such education requires control by the
state. Thus (J.3), (J.4), and (J.5). This combination of factors also provides moral justification for the minority to rule over the majority during
the time necessary to reshape them. Legitimation of minority rule requires a distinction between the "empirical" interests of the majority,
what they *believe* they want or what they want at the present time, and
their "real" interests, what they would want if they had not been corrupted by existing society and so what they will want once they have been

properly educated and understand the benefits of the perfect society. Although the majority has not consented to being ruled by the minority and would not consent if they were given the opportunity, at some unspecified future time they will be grateful for having been ruled and will consent retrospectively. This particular set of ideas, expressed in (J.6), is frequently not recognized by theorists, and so I will pay relatively little attention to it. As discussion in previous chapters indicates, I am mainly concerned with (J.3), the nature of the elite minority, and (J.4) and (J.5), how they are to attain political power and how this will be used to accomplish their educative ends. These ideas of course influence one another and are also strongly affected by (J.1), the nature of the ideal society. It is to this interrelated set of ideas that I now turn.

ROBESPIERRE AS POLITICAL THEORIST

The most important Jacobin figure during the French Revolution was Maximilien Robespierre, who was the main spokesperson for the revolutionary government under the Committee of Public Safety during the pivotal year 1793–94—the year of the Terror, or the Year II, according to the new revolutionary calendar. The original Jacobins were members of political clubs. The Society of the Friends of the Constitution was formed in 1789 and got its nickname because it met in a former Dominican convent, the members of which were known as Jacobins. The Paris Club and its numerous affiliates throughout France were notable for radical views. During the reign of the Committee of Public Safety, they became unofficial arms of the government, involved in watch committees and revolutionary tribunals. In his classic study of the Jacobins, Crane Brinton estimates that at their peak there were some 6,800 Jacobin clubs established throughout France.[6] Though membership is difficult to determine, Brinton estimates that the societies had some five hundred thousand committed members during the time of the Terror, or about 2 percent of the population. Total membership over the course of the Revolution was some one million.[7]

In early 1793 the Revolution was under siege. France was at war with Prussia, Austria, and Britain, faring poorly on the battlefield and unable to count on the loyalty of its generals. Civil war raged in several provinces, the inhabitants of which took up arms against the revolutionary government. To respond to emergency conditions, the National Convention placed governmental power in the hands of two committees: the Committee of Public Safety and the Committee of General Security. The former, especially, came to exercise something approaching dictatorial authority. The Constitution of 1793, drafted for the new Republic, was set aside before it could be implemented. On October 10, 1793, the Convention declared that the provisional government of France would be "revolutionary until the peace." The Committee of Public Safety eventually came to have twelve members. Robespierre was placed on it on July 27, 1793, and served for almost exactly a year, until his fall on July 27, 1794, and execution the following day.

Robespierre is one of the great enigmatic figures of modern history. Interpretations of his character and motives range from the dictatorial fiend of conservative historians—"the most hateful character in the forefront of history since Machiavelli reduced to a code the wickedness of public men"—to the fearsome figure of the incorruptible republican—the "Seagreen" incorruptible of Carlyle[8]—to the sainted pioneer of social democracy made popular by Alfred Mathiez, perhaps his greatest champion.[9] An indication of the difficulty of coming to terms with Robespierre is that Norman Hampson constructed his recent biography in the form of a dialogue between himself and representatives of three alternative points of view: a civil servant, a Communist, and a clergyman.[10]

The nature of the evidence poses impediments to a definitive interpretation. Aside from always difficult problems of determining motivation, Robespierre expressed his views in a number of speeches delivered in the National Assembly and the Convention and to the Jacobin Club. This wealth of material, never systematically developed in treatise form, allows the commentator considerable license to pick and choose quotations and so to construe Robespierre's views in a variety of ways.[11] These problems are compounded by the fact that Robespierre was a political figure. His speeches lend themselves to different interpretations: as sincere expressions of his views or, on the opposite extreme, as presented primarily for tactical reasons, to advance some policy or other or to outmaneuver political rivals. The speeches, moreover, might not be expressions of Robespierre's views at all, as many, including some of the most important, were presented in his capacity as representing the Committee of Public Safety to either the Convention or the Jacobins. But in spite of apparent inconsistencies in the views expressed before and after he ascended to the Committee (on which more below), the consistency of central themes in Robespierre's speeches supports the interpretation that they expressed his own convictions.[12] This view is supported, on more subjective grounds, by the power and eloquence of Robespierre's expression, which strikes the reader — or at least this reader — as from the heart. As Mathiez says, in spite of unprepossessing appearance and a weak voice, Robespierre was able to govern France through the sheer force of his eloquence. Mathiez refers to him as "eloquence personified."[13] To my mind, the elegance and eloquence of Robespierre's language is comparable to that of Edmund Burke's declamations, on the other side of the great political issues of the time.

I concentrate mainly on a set of important addresses Robespierre gave in 1793–94, although I draw on others as well. These concern the principles of revolutionary government (December 25, 1793), the principles of the Republic's political morality (February 5, 1794), the cult of the Supreme Being (May 7, 1794), Robespierre's last address to the Convention (July 26, 1794), and public education (July 29, 1793). With the possible exception of the last named (but first delivered), these are among Robespierre's most important and best-known addresses. Although different scholars would expand the list by including additional speeches, there is little doubt about the centrality of these.[14]

It is important to recognize that the fundamental ideas expressed in this body of material extend beyond ideas peculiar to Robespierre. Central themes were common to other members of the Mountain — the left-wing faction in the Convention (and the origin of left-wing/right-wing political terminology) — and other members of the Committee of Public Safety, especially Louis-Antoine de Saint-Just. Although Saint-Just differed from Robespierre on important points,[15] the two men were in basic agreement on fundamental matters, including public education. I will appeal to Saint-Just from time to time to flesh out Robespierre's views and will examine below some of Saint-Just's ideas on the institutions of a properly constituted republic.

The deep structure of Robespierre's political thought is based on a few fundamental premises.[16] First is belief in the existence of true, ultimate moral principles. There are eternal verities, he said in 1791, which are "maxims of justice, universal, unalterable, imprescriptible, made to be applied to all peoples" (quoted in Cobban, p. 137). As Alfred Cobban says, Robespierre's idea of universally valid, objective moral principles places him in the natural law tradition (Cobban, p. 137).

In a virtuous government, these principles will be given free rein. Robespierre follows Montesquieu and Rousseau in identifying virtue with subordination of private interests to the public interest. In a properly constituted state, virtue will reign and along with it happiness. In 1784 Robespierre said that "virtue produces happiness as the sun produces light" (Cobban, p. 138).

Robespierre also follows the natural law tradition in believing that moral truths are accessible to human beings, written on men's hearts. Thus he subscribes to Rousseau's faith that the people are naturally good, a view that made him a strong proponent of popular sovereignty. If the people are good, a republican government, in which they rule themselves, is necessary. The problems of corrupt polities, then, can be alleviated if the people are able to rule themselves, subordinating their private interests to the public interest, which is in accord with eternal verities. As Robespierre said in 1793: "It is in the virtue and sovereignty of the people that it is necessary to find a preservative against the vices and despotism of government" (Cobban, p. 138).

In enunciating two basic political desiderata, Robespierre opens the way for considerable tension. In a happy and virtuous republic, the people rule themselves, placing the public good over individual concerns, a circumstance that also promotes objective moral values. Faith in this combination of elements underlay earlier phases of Robespierre's career. He originally made his name as an ardent democrat by standing with the people in opposition to attempts to contain the consequences of the Revolution. Thus, early in the Revolution, he argued against attempts of the Legislative Assembly to deny the right to vote to large segments of the population and opposed France's going to war with the other European powers, fearing that this would lead to a situation in which a military dictator could emerge and subvert the Revolution.[17] Robespierre's extreme democratic views

during the early years of the Revolution propelled him to political promi-
nence and power. However, when he was in power and popular demands
came into conflict with what he believed to be necessary governmental policies, he was led to qualify his support of popular rule in important ways.

There is an obvious tension in Robespierre's thought between what
the people want—assuming, counterfactually, that the French people were
a homogeneous entity—and what Robespierre believed to be necessary
and in keeping with objectively valid principles. As long as these two sets
of demands coincided, Robespierre was not forced to choose between
them. This condition was satisfied most readily when Robespierre was in a
position of opposition, combating less democratic elements in the government. But for our purposes, his ideas became more interesting when the
two demands came into conflict. To the extent that he retained faith in
the people's virtue and goodness, Robespierre's thought departs from
Jacobin theory, as laid out earlier in this chapter. If the people can be
trusted to rule themselves, there is no need for an enlightened elite or minority to seize political power and use it to educate them. Thus Robespierre became a Jacobin in our sense only when he lost faith in the people's
worth and aspirations. The shifting currents in Robespierre's thought
throughout his career should most likely be viewed as attempts to pursue
his ultimate values under evolving political circumstances, which called
for different tactics. Most important was his eventual realization that the
people could not be relied on always to pursue their own best interests.

From his position in the Committee of Public Safety, Robespierre
tried various tacks to deal with the people's corruption. While in the Committee, he supported government by a minority who represented them,
were required to act on their behalf, and also should undertake the task of
properly educating them. More familiar—and notorious—were his ideas
concerning the need to purge corrupt elements of the populace, to preserve the people's purity.

Revolutionary Government

Robespierre conceived of the goal of revolutionary politics in extraordi-
narily lofty terms. The clearest expression of this aspiration is his great

speech on the principles of the Republic's political morality, delivered on February 5, 1794:[18]

> What is the end at which we aim? The peaceable enjoyment of liberty and equality; the reign of that eternal justice, the laws of which are not written on marble or stone, but on the hearts of all men, even that of the slave who forgets them and the tyrant who denies them.
>
> We want an order of things where all base and cruel passions are enchained by the laws, all beneficent and generous passions awakened; where ambition is the desire to deserve glory and to serve one's country; where distinctions arise only from equality itself; where the citizen is subject to the magistrate, the magistrate to the people, the people to justice; where the country guarantees the welfare of each individual, and each individual proudly enjoys the prosperity and glory of his country; where all souls are enlarged by the constant communication of republican sentiments and by the need to earn the esteem of a great people; where the arts are decorations of liberty, which ennobles them; commerce is the source of public wealth, not simply of monstrous riches for a few families.
>
> We want to substitute in our land morality for egotism, probity for a mere sense of honor, principle for custom, duty for propriety, the empire of reason for the tyranny of fashion, contempt for vice for contempt for misfortune, pride for insolence, large-mindedness for vanity, the love of glory for the love of money, good people for good company, merit for intrigue, talent for mere wit, truth for show, the charm of happiness for the tedium of pleasure, the grandeur of man for the pettiness of grand society, a people magnanimous, powerful and happy for a people likable, frivolous and wretched—that is to say, all the virtues and all the miracles of the Republic for all the vices and puerilities of the monarchy.
>
> We want in a word to fulfill the course of nature, to accomplish the destiny of mankind, to make good the promises of philosophy, to absolve Providence from the long reign of crime and tyranny. May France, formerly illustrious among enslaved peoples, eclipse the glory of all free peoples that have existed, become the model to the nations, the terror of oppressors, the consolation of the oppressed, the

ornament of the universe; and in sealing our work with our blood may we be able to see at least the dawn of universal felicity gleam before us! That is our ambition. That is our aim. (*Oeuvres,* X, 352)

I have quoted Robespierre at length to give some idea of his expression, the force of which increases with accumulation of details. As one can see, Robespierre depicts a semblance of paradise. It is not easy to think of another political figure who expressed his aspirations in such exalted terms while in power and able to take concrete steps to realize them. However, if Robespierre's goals seem excessive, one should keep in mind that he was not alone in extravagant aspirations. Far from it. For example, the Revolution abolished the Christian calendar to begin anew. After the Convention authorized a new calendar—divided not into seven-day weeks but into ten-day *décadi*—September 22, 1791, the date on which the Convention convened, was declared the first day of the Year I.

While on the Committee of Public Safety, Robespierre was first and foremost a political actor, taking steps to deal with the extraordinary concatenation of problems the times offered up: not only war abroad and civil war at home, but the restiveness of the Parisian population demanding economic relief. Although not organized into formal political parties, the Convention was divided into factions with different views about how to deal with these problems. Robespierre and the others members of the Committee of Public Safety had to retain the support of the Convention, a working relationship with the Committee of General Security, and the support of the Parisian populace, whose revolutionary initiative had sparked the Revolution, overthrown the monarchy, and purged the Convention, placing the Mountain in control. To meet these demands, the Committee of Public Safety oversaw the first modern, totally mobilized society. The *levée en masse* raised an army of a million men, supported by a centrally controlled economy and the enforcement mechanisms of revolutionary justice. The popular surveillance committees and revolutionary tribunals too were eventually brought under centralized control, in the hands of the Committee of Public Safety.[19]

Forced to react to a continually shifting political landscape, Robespierre did not have the luxury of indulging in academic political theory.

Although his speeches probably reflect his own convictions, the policies he supported were largely dictated by day-to-day events, as opposed to being parts of a master plan, directed primarily toward a clearly envisioned central goal.[20]

As a political theorist, Robespierre was perhaps most innovative in justifying government by the Committee of Public Safety and so the fact that the Revolution had brought forth dictatorship. In the early stages of his career, he was a strong proponent of the people and advocated their participation in politics. Thus he also supported their right to resist oppression. But as a member of the Committee, Robespierre took a different view of popular opposition to governmental actions. Tight control of power was necessary until the enemies of the Revolution had been vanquished and also to place the people in a position in which they could rule themselves. Although Robespierre believed that the people were naturally good, they had been "degraded by the vices of our former social system" (*Oeuvres,* X, 12). With the people corrupted by the ancien régime, the Revolution was "attempting to raise the temple of liberty with hands still stained by the chains of despotism" (quoted in Cobban, p. 172). In order for the Revolution to succeed, the people must be enlightened. Robespierre assigned the revolutionary government the twin tasks of suppressing the Revolution's foes and raising the people to virtue. As we will see, these two sides of the Committee's task were linked in Robespierre's mind, because he tended to view the Republic's enemies as responsible for its plight.

Robespierre's account of revolutionary government is set forth in his great speech of December 25, 1793. He begins by proclaiming the novelty of his doctrine:

> The theory of revolutionary government is as new as the Revolution that created it. One cannot look for it in the books of the political theorists, who completely failed to foresee this revolution, nor in the laws of the tyrants who, content to abuse their power, do not bother themselves with its legal justification. (*Oeuvres,* X, 274)

He continues with an account of revolutionary government's purpose, justifying the extraordinary powers of the Committee of Public Safety:

The function of government is to guide the moral and physical energies of the nation toward the purposes for which it was established.

The aim of constitutional government is to preserve the Republic; the aim of revolutionary government is to establish it.

Revolution is the war waged by liberty against its enemies; the constitution is the reign of liberty, with victory won and the regime at peace. (*Oeuvres*, X, 274)

For the Revolution to succeed, its enemies must be defeated. These include not only the foreign powers abroad with whom France was at war but also treasonous elements of the population. I have noted that the revolutionary government was beset by civil wars in the Vendée, Lyons, and elsewhere. But the Republic's enemies extended beyond even these purviews. Conspirators abounded, and combating them required drastic means: The revolutionary government's power to repress must be commensurate "with the audacity or perfidy of those who conspire against it" (X, 275).

The existence of a great conspiracy of the Revolution's enemies is one of Robespierre's central themes during his time on the Committee of Public Safety. Up to a point, his fear was rooted in reality. Aristocrats and monarchists opposed the Revolution, and foreign powers had agents throughout France. But a good part of Robespierre's preoccupation with traitors can be attributed to his Manichaean view of the world and, undoubtedly, deep paranoia. Robespierre viewed a conspiracy of opponents of the Revolution in France allied with opponents abroad and attributed impediments to the Revolution's success to this all-embracing opposition.

Throughout his career, Robespierre attributed the Republic's problems to traitors. Although he believed the people's intentions were always pure, they were easily misled. In February 1793 he wrote: "The mistakes of the people are few and transient, always the product of the fatality of circumstances or the crime of perverted individuals."[21] This attitude was reflected in various policy pronouncements. Having scant knowledge of economic theory or how economies worked, Robespierre traced food shortages and other economic problems to hoarders and speculators. Food riots were instigated by foreign powers, to discredit the Revolution.[22]

Though he had staunchly supported freedom of the press, Robespierre came to see this as a great danger. The people must be enlightened, but the greatest obstacle to progress on this front was the "paid journalists, who mislead it every day by shameless impostures"; "It is necessary to proscribe these writers as the most dangerous enemies of the country."[23]

Most serious, Robespierre came to see political opposition to the policies of the Committee of Public Safety as evidence of treason. Radical elements of the Parisian populace demanded further economic measures to alleviate the plight of the working class and in regard to de-Christianization. But on the other hand, as revolutionary armies achieved success against enemies both abroad and at home, elements of the government wished to ease up on the Terror and economic controls. The danger of veering off in either direction is a constant theme in Robespierre's speeches. To pursue the former course is to risk alienating conservative rural populations and so to revive the popular revolts that had just been suppressed. To pursue the latter is to weaken the Revolution's ability to function. Justice delayed amounts to protecting the guilty from punishment and so safety for the tyrant and his allies. In his address on political morality, Robespierre moves from depicting the ends of the Revolution and the principles of revolutionary government in general terms to assailing the two wings of this counterrevolutionary army. In spite of their differences, the two camps of false revolutionaries follow policies dictated "by committees of Prussians, English, Austrians, even Muscovites" (*Oeuvres,* X, 360).

According to Robespierre, the aim of the Revolution is to establish the Republic, a government in which the people rule. But in spite of his never wavering faith in the people's natural virtue, he became increasingly restrictive in regard to exactly who fell under the honorific category "the people." Even early in the Revolution, Robespierre never included all individuals but only members of the third estate, opposed to the privileged classes. Within the third estate, he distinguished between the people proper and the wealthy bourgeoisie (Cobban, pp. 186–87). As the Revolution progressed, the people became more exclusive. In December 1793 he said: "All reasonable and magnanimous men are the party of the Republic; all perfidious and corrupt individuals are the party of your tyrants" (quoted in Cobban, p. 187). In the great speech of February 5,

1794: "Society owes protection only to peaceable citizens; the only citizens in the Republic are the republicans. The royalists, the conspirators are only strangers, or rather, enemies" (*Oeuvres*, X, 357). In May 1794:

> There are two peoples in France, the one is the mass of citizens, pure and simple, moved by justice and lovers of liberty. These are the virtuous people who spill their blood to establish liberty, who prevail over enemies within and topple the thrones of tyrants. The other is the collection of factions and intriguers. (Quoted in Cobban, p. 187)

The latter mislead the people, extolling the ancient regime, and attempting to dominate public opinion. In keeping with his Manichaean tendencies, Robespierre excludes these groups from "the people": "I know of only two parties, the party of good citizens and the party of bad" (*Oeuvres*, X, 551). For the latter, the consequences are severe: "To good citizens revolutionary government owes the full protection of the nation; to the enemies of the people it owes only death" (X, 274).

To Robespierre, the Revolution meant establishing liberty and defeating its foes. Reformulating Montesquieu's idea that the principle or motivating force of the republic is virtue, he argues:

> If the spring of popular government in time of peace is virtue, the springs of popular government in revolution are at once *virtue and terror:* virtue, without which terror is fatal; terror, without which virtue is powerless. (*Oeuvres*, X, 357; original emphasis)

Castigating deliberate judicial proceedings, Robespierre lays out a theoretical defense of the Reign of Terror:[24] To deal with treason, delay could be fatal. The sword of justice must be swift and deadly.

The logical conclusion of this point of view was the law of the 22d Prairial (June 10, 1794—two days after the Festival of the Supreme Being). This law, which Robespierre was instrumental in pushing through, greatly reduced legal protections of accused persons. According to the law: "The Revolutionary Tribunal is instituted to punish the enemies of the people." It decreed that the only sentence the Revolutionary Tribunal could impose was death. The law also greatly reduced legal and procedural protections for accused persons.[25] With passage of the law, the number of executions rose dramatically. Between April 1, 1793, and June 10, 1794, the date of the law, the Revolutionary Tribunal passed 1,254 death sentences. Between June 10 and July 27 — the day of Robespierre's fall — it passed 1,258, as many in those few weeks as in the previous fourteen months.[26]

The law of 22d Prairial is fully in keeping with Robespierre's views on the principle of revolutionary government:

> Terror is nothing other than justice, prompt, severe, inflexible; it is therefore an emanation of virtue; it is not so much a particular principle as a consequence of the general principle of democracy applied to the most pressing needs of our country. (*Oeuvres*, X, 357)

The great danger, of course, is that this form of justice invites abuse. Extraordinary circumstances demand extraordinary powers, but how can one guarantee that these will not be misused? Robespierre's answer is virtue. If virtue is subordination of private interests to the public good, governmental functionaries above all must be moved by this sentiment: "The higher the source of public order is raised, the purer it ought to be." The Convention, which authorizes the governing committees and other bodies, must take special care to guarantee its own virtue: "[T]he representative body, then, must begin amongst itself by subduing all private passions to the general passion for the public good" (*Oeuvres*, X, 356). As Robespierre said in his last speech to the Convention: "The arms of liberty must be touched only by pure hands" (X, 557); "[T]he characteristic of popular government is confidence in the people and severity against itself" (X, 356).

The great paradox in Robespierre's insistence on the purity of revolutionary government is that this legitimizes further purges of the government and so makes central control of the levers of power even more dangerous. Tellingly, the law of 22d Prairial also withdrew protection from arrest by Convention members, although the day after it was passed the Convention voted to reinstate this.[27] But given past history, the threat was clear, a situation exacerbated to no end by the conviction that disagreement was prima facie evidence of treason. As we have seen, to wish to moderate the government's policies is treason, as is to wish to intensify them. Not only are such deviations helpful to the Revolution's foes, but their proponents must be in the pay of foreign governments. Although Robespierre and other members of the revolutionary government were well aware of the importance of maintaining unity in the governing committees, this became impossible. Repeated purges led to mutual suspicion and political differences fought out in life-and-death struggles. Elimination of the Girondins, the Hebertists, and Danton and his associates heightened the overall atmosphere of fear and mistrust. In his final speech to the Convention, Robespierre claimed to have uncovered another plot:

> Let us say there exists a conspiracy against public liberty; that it owes its force to a criminal coalition intriguing within the very bosom of the Convention; that this coalition has accomplices in the Committee of General Security and in the bureaus of that Committee, which it dominates; . . . that members of the Committee of Public Safety have taken part in this plot. (*Oeuvres*, X, 576)

To remedy this situation, Robespierre demanded another purge, "a clean sweep of the bureaus of the Committee of General Security," which should be subordinated to the Committee of Public Safety. A purge of that Committee would result in a unified government under the National Convention. "[T]o crush all the factions with the weight of the national authority, to raise on their ruins the power of justice and liberty." These are the principles that must be followed (X, 576).

Scholars generally believe that Robespierre committed a serious political error in this speech in not identifying his targets by name. Many members of the Committees and the Convention felt threatened, and this contributed to his arrest the next day and subsequent execution. But there was an inescapable flaw in his idea that governmental virtue could be preserved by purges. Had Robespierre prevailed in this particular conflict and crushed "all the factions," this would not have been the end of conflict. Additional disagreements undoubtedly would have arisen and so the need for still additional purges.

In his speech to the Convention denouncing Danton and his colleagues, Saint-Just forecasted a time when only patriots would remain and no more purges would be necessary: "After the factions have been abolished, endow the republic with gentle *moeurs*. Reestablish esteem and respect for the individual in civil society." The French people should be happy and free, they should love themselves, hate their enemies, and live in mutual peace: "Liberty is calling you back to nature."[28] But of course this was not the last purge. After Danton's faction was crushed, others arose, until Saint-Just too was purged along with Robespierre. The cycle of purges ended only with the Thermidorean reaction, which brought the Terror to an end but also the radical hopes of the Revolution.

THE POLITICS OF REGENERATION

In addition to his account of revolutionary government and justification of its extraordinary powers, Robespierre theorized about other means to attain his idealized ends. He supported public education and civic religion to make the people fit to constitute a new society. This side of his political theory is less familiar—and less developed—than what we have seen but central to his philosophy of radical reform.

Robespierre's ideas on education and public religion help to fill in the sketch of an ideal society noted above. He took an active role in formulating educational policy for the Revolution as one of six commissioners appointed to address educational questions. He reported to the Convention on July 13 and 29, 1793, but did so by reading a plan for national education composed by Louis-Michel Lepelletier. Lepelletier had been a member of the Convention who, after voting to execute the King, was assassinated in January 1793 by a royalist fanatic. Among his papers was found the educational plan that Robespierre read.

According to Robespierre, public education was needed to renew the French people:

[C]onsidering the point to which the human species has been degraded by the vices of our former social system, I am convinced of the necessity of effecting a complete regeneration and, if I might express myself thus, of creating a new people. (*Oeuvres,* X, 12)

Public education was one of the three monuments the Convention would leave to history, along with the Constitution and a code of civil laws (*Oeuvres,* X, 12). Although Robespierre noted that he preferred a still more far-reaching plan, Lepelletier's was highly ambitious. It would provide a system of education for all children, regardless of family income. Its impetus was clearly Spartan. Under public education, "the whole being of the child" belongs to the Republic (*Oeuvres,* X, 24). All children would be removed from their homes and sent to public boarding schools, boys between the ages of five and twelve and girls between five and eleven.

Distinguishing between education of the character and instruction of the mind, Robespierre concentrated on the former. The heart of the proposal was comprehensive physical and mental training, "under the holy law of equality," all children receiving "the same clothes, the same food, the same instruction, the same care" (X, 15). Children would receive instruction in reading and writing and learn patriotic songs, the history of free peoples and of the Revolution. Much of the education would be practical; working with their hands would be students' principal occupation. Boys would work on roads or factories and girls learn needlepoint and to do laundry. During a transition period of four years, enrollment was to be voluntary. After that parents who refused to turn their children over to the common schools would lose their civil rights and pay additional taxes.

The period between the ages of five and twelve is "decisive for the formation of one's physical and moral being" (*Oeuvres,* X, 15). After this stage children would continue through additional stages of education, the details of which need not concern us. More important is the principal aim of Lepelletier's and Robespierre's scheme, which is moral training dedicated to the inculcation of virtue. With proper virtues instilled in the citizenry, the Republic would see a doubling of agricultural and industrial production. Crime would disappear and the Republic reap additional advantages. Unless all citizens receive proper education, "the nation will not be able to be profoundly regenerated" (X, 22).

Lepelletier's proposals were debated by the Convention, and a modified version was adopted in August 1793. An important revision weakened mandatory attendance requirements in order to address rural parents' need for their children's assistance with agricultural labor. But even so modified, the scheme was far too ambitious for the times. It was never put into practice and was rescinded by the Convention on October 20, 1793.[29]

Robespierre's other major proposal for moral regeneration was based on civic religion and public festivals. His central ideas strongly resemble Rousseau's prescriptions in Book IV of the *Social Contract*. Like Rousseau, Robespierre proposed general belief in the existence of a Supreme Being and the immortality of the soul and religious toleration beyond that.

His speech of May 7, 1794, "The Relation of Religion and Morality to Republican Principles,"[30] was in response to antireligious excesses of revolutionary zealots, who moved beyond attacking the Catholic Church to assail religion altogether. Robespierre defended both religion's truth and its social utility. "The moral world, even more than the physical world," he began, "seems full of contrasts and enigmas" (*Oeuvres*, X, 443). In contrast to the great accomplishments of civilization in the natural world in which man is coming to master nature, in the moral world people seem unaware of the "principal ideas of public morality" (X, 444). The enemies of the Revolution had elevated immorality into a system, attempting to suppress all noble and generous sentiments. Because belief in the existence of God exalts man's being and elevates his heart, atheism is "linked to a system of conspiracy against the Republic" (X, 452). "In the eyes of the legislator, truth is all that is useful and of practical good in the world. The idea of the Supreme Being and immortality of the soul is a continual summons to justice; it is therefore social and republican" (X, 452). Inculcating these beliefs will further instinctive tendencies to do good. Because religious respect for men grounds men's duties and "is the only guarantor of social happiness," it must be promoted through all institutions. Appealing to the experiences of Greece and Rome, as he did frequently throughout the speech, Robespierre invoked the ideas of public festivals, which he regarded as "an essential part of public education" (X, 458). "A system of national festivals of course would be at the same time the most pleasant bond of brotherhood and the most powerful means of regeneration" (X, 459).

To advance his religious ideas, Robespierre concluded his address with a decree, consisting of fifteen articles. These included the assertion that "[t]he French people recognize the existence of the Supreme Being and the immortality of the soul" but also that the best way to worship the Supreme Being is to do one's duties and defend freedom of worship. Festivals were also proposed "to remind men of the Deity and the worth of his being." The festivals were to be named after glorious events of the Revolution, the virtues, and the blessings of nature. On successive *décadis,* festivals were to celebrate the Supreme Being, Nature, the human race, the French people, and an entire list of entities, including good faith, love, filial piety, childhood, youth, manhood, old age, and misfortune (*Oeuvres,* X, 462–65).

Although Robespierre's speech on the Supreme Being bears the clear stamp of his personality, its basic ideas were widely shared in the Convention. On its completion, Robespierre's associate, Couthon, demanded that the discourse be widely circulated throughout France, posted in all streets, "translated into all the languages and spread throughout the entire universe."[31] Members of the Convention supported going farther than Robespierre. While Rousseau had supported banishing people who did not accept his civil faith, on this point Robespierre demurred. But a Paris delegate named Julien supported banishment. In response, Robespierre argued that such a provision would inspire too much fear in "a multitude of imbeciles and corrupt men." It should be left in Rousseau's text and not be put into practice.[32]

The fifteen articles of the decree were adopted by the Convention. Robespierre was elected president of the body and in that capacity presided over a magnificent public festival in honor of the Supreme Being. Planned by the artist Jacques-Louis David, the festivities included a procession of cavalry and drummers, men and women garlanded with oak leaves, all members of the Convention carrying bouquets of wheat, flowers and fruit, an oxcart hauling a collection of symbolic objects: a sheaf of grain, a printing press, a young oak tree, and a statue of liberty. There was also an enormous artificial mountain, symbolizing the Republic, on which stood selected citizens while members of the Convention climbed to the summit.[33] At the festival's culmination, Robespierre made a brief, sermonlike address. He approached a symbolic figure of Atheism and set it on fire with a torch. Atheism disappeared "into nothingness," and from the ashes rose an image of Wisdom.[34]

SAINT-JUST'S REPUBLICAN INSTITUTIONS

Like Robespierre, Saint-Just has gone down in history as an apostle of terror. Robespierre's consistent ally on the Committee of Public Safety, Saint-Just gave public expression to some of its most aggressive pronouncements. For example, it was he who addressed the Convention on October 10, 1793, on the need to declare the government "revolutionary until the peace." On February 26, 1794, he said: "What constitutes a republic is the total destruction of whatever is opposed to it" (*Oeuvres*, p. 700). Saint-Just delivered the prosecutorial speech before the Convention, laying out the crimes of Danton and his associates—while reportedly making chopping motions with his arm, like the blade of a guillotine.[35] The October 10 speech contains one of Saint-Just's most famous pronouncements:

> We cannot hope for prosperity while the last enemy of liberty still breathes. You must punish not only the traitors but even those who are indifferent; you must punish whoever is passive in the Republic and does nothing for her; because once the French people have made known their will, everything that is opposed to it is outside the sovereign; whatever is outside the sovereign is enemy. (*Oeuvres*, p. 521)

However, there is another side to Saint-Just. Like Robespierre, he was a proponent of virtue as well as terror, but he went much farther than Robespierre in outlining an ideal regime in which virtue would be fostered. Sometime in 1794 the Committee of Public Safety commissioned one of its members, presumably Saint-Just, to draft a plan of "republican institutions." Fragments were eventually found in Saint-Just's papers. Although these are incomplete, amounting to some forty pages in his *Collected Works* (*Oeuvres*, pp. 966–1009), they are sufficient to convey a good idea of his plans for developing suitable citizens for a virtuous republic—as well as of his overall cast of mind.

It is not possible to date Saint-Just's *Institutions* with precision. The fragments may well have been composed at different times. Portions appear to have been intended for a revised version of Saint-Just's early work, *De la nature*.[36] But it is not unlikely that Saint-Just discussed the ideas the fragments contain with friends and associates, especially Robespierre. Although Saint-Just's specific proposals strike the reader as impossibly archaic and utopian, we should note that important details show the influence of prominent educational theorizing of the times, especially the views of Lepelletier.[37]

By the notion of "institutions," Saint-Just meant "the gradual formation of moral and civic habits through organized expression."[38] Like Plato and other ancient thinkers, Saint-Just believed that people's conduct is decisively affected by their habits and mores and so by the conditions under which they are raised. Systematic molding of citizens is central to the virtuous republic. The purpose of republican institutions is stated at the opening of the work: "Institutions are the guaranty of the government of a free people against corruption of their *moeurs,* and the guaranty of the people and citizens against the corruption of government" (*Oeuvres,* p. 967). Proper institutions are necessary for the establishment of the republic: "Terror is able to overthrow the monarch and aristocracy, but what will deliver us from corruption?" The answer: "Institutions" (p. 976). They are the means through which citizens' characters can be transformed. They are intended to inculcate frugality and courage, to render citizens just and sensitive, to "put the public interest in place of all other interests, to strangle criminal passion and to develop nature and innocence as the passions in all hearts and to form a commonwealth" (pp. 967–68). This summary leaves out items on Saint-Just's list, but it gives an idea of the scope of his intended aims.

The main topics covered in Saint-Just's *Institutions* are education, friendship, and some other domestic practices. In spite of the unfinished state of the manuscript, it is sufficient to show the deep influence of Spartan and other ancient polities on Saint-Just's thought. As noted, his views on education are similar to Lepelletier's, but they are more extreme: "Children belong to their mother, if she has nursed them, until they are five and to the republic from then on until their death" (p. 982). Children are to be educated in common, removed from their homes, and organized in companies, under rigorous discipline. They will engage in infantry and cavalry maneuvers and learn languages. They will live on bread, vegetables, dairy products, and water, be dressed in linen all year long, and will not return to their parents until the age of twenty-one. During harvest time, they will be sent to labor in the fields—perhaps in recognition of the problems Robespierre's and Lepelletier's plan encountered in the Convention (*Oeuvres,* pp. 981–82). From twenty-one to twenty-five, men are to perform military service, although Saint-Just appears not to have thought through the economic consequences of maintaining and equipping an enormous standing army.[39] Saint-Just repeatedly invokes the ideal of inducing *laconisme* in students' speech; point-by-point comparisons with Plutarch's description of Spartan practices makes the overall resemblance apparent.[40]

Also drawn from ancient times—in this case, presumably, Rome—is the institution of censors, although this is described more briefly. Men who have lived without reproach will be given a white sash to wear at the age of sixty. They will then have the power to censure the private lives of those under twenty-one years of age and the private conduct of public officials (*Oeuvres,* p. 985).

In regard to matters of religion, Saint-Just's ideas closely approximate Robespierre's. "The French people recognize the Supreme Being and the immortality of the soul." The first day of every month will be consecrated to the eternal. But there is to be freedom of religion. All cults are to be permitted and protected and the public temples open to all. However, priests are not to appear in public in their religious vestments, on pain of banishment. Temples are to be open day and night, never closed. The people are to chant the hymn to the eternal every morning; all public festivals will begin with this hymn (p. 984).

Though the *Institutions* does not contain a worked out economic program, there are hints of one scattered throughout the manuscript. Rough economic equality will be promoted. Servants will dine in common with their masters. Every tenth day, citizens will eat in common. No one will be allowed to cultivate more than 300 arpents (about 300 acres). Everyone will pay a tax of 10 percent of his income, which will go toward a public domain, to be used to help the unfortunate and reward those who have performed great services for society. Some economic ideas are clearly eccentric. Landowners must keep one sheep for every arpent, an ox for every ten, and a horse for every fifteen. Capital cannot be invested abroad, but otherwise citizens are free to do with their wealth as they please, although each year they must give a public accounting of what they have done with their fortunes.

Perhaps the most unusual of Saint-Just's institutions is friendship. At the age of twenty-one every man must declare in the temple the names of his friends and must renew that declaration every year. Friends will be placed side by side in combat. They are not allowed to enter into written contracts with one another or to sue one another. If someone commits a crime, his friends are banished. If someone wishes to drop a friend, he must explain this publicly, again in the temple. But those who remain friends their entire lives are buried in the same tomb. If someone declares that he does not believe in friendship or does not have friends, he is banished (pp. 983–84).

Saint-Just's eccentric treatment of friendship was influenced by the Spartan custom of companions dining together at public messes and then fighting side by side, or perhaps the Theban Sacred Band. There is a certain ingenuity in the attempt to strengthen civic ties by drawing on additional emotions.[41] But it does not require great insight to realize that his proposals could not possibly work in a large nation-state. Perhaps in a small, closed society, divided into exclusive clans, one could maintain the same group of friends throughout life, without the network of overlapping friendships and associations that would eventually involve almost everyone.[42]

The virtuous republic is also to be furthered by coercive means. Throughout the *Institutions,* Saint-Just prescribes banishment as the penalty for an entire litany of crimes. We have seen that banishment enforces the institution of friendship. But in addition, whoever strikes a child is banished (p. 980). Whoever deceives a girl is banished (p. 983). A public official convicted of wickedness is banished. If someone vandalizes graves or censures the conduct of others, he is banished. Whoever commits an offense while drunk is banished (p. 985). And so on.

The death penalty is also frequently invoked. This applies to people who try to defy their banishment, or murderers who fail to wear the black clothing required of them for the rest of their lives. The penalty is also death for someone who strikes a woman or hits someone in a temple, for officers who strike their men, or women who frequent army camps.

This extensive list of what we can call penalties of elimination illumi-
nates the darker side of Saint-Just's attempt to construct an ideal society.
His reputation as a supporter of extreme measures shows forth in the
Institutions. Echoing Robespierre, Saint-Just preaches the need for terror
as well as virtue: "A republican government has virtue for its principle; if
not, terror" (p. 978). His two-pronged approach is to turn the citizenry
toward virtue and eliminate what resists.

It does not seem controversial to say that in many ways Saint-Just's
Republican Institutions is an absurd work, or sketch of a work, utterly out
of keeping with its times. According to Frank Manuel and Fritzie Manuel,
Saint-Just, along with Robespierre, was "one of the last of the great static
utopians of calm felicity." His ideal vision was "of a state impervious to
time and corruption, under an ideal of unchanging or virtually unchanging laws."[43] Hampson describes the *Institutions* as "the culminating point
in [the author's] retreat from reality into a world of myth and retribu-
tion."[44] Whether one chooses such a view or Brinton's claim that the
work must be understood as an example of religious fanaticism,[45] it is unsettling to realize that it was to some degree authorized by the Committee
of Public Safety. There is little doubt about Saint-Just's seriousness:
"The day on which I become convinced that it is impossible to give the
French people *moeurs* that are gentle, energetic, sensitive, and inexorable
against tyranny and injustice, I will stab myself" (p. 977).

Utopian Means

Let us return to the question of establishing the ideal society. Robespierre
and to a lesser extent Saint-Just address this subject, although we should
recognize that neither provides detailed or explicit treatment. Writing
during the turmoil of the Revolution, Robespierre and Saint-Just were
forced to deal with recurrent crises and so, unlike the theorists discussed
in previous chapters, did not have the luxury of engaging in pure theory
about the movement to future society. Both theorists, moreover, were more
important as political actors than political theorists. Robespierre's ideas,
though original in significant respects and wonderfully expressed, do not
constitute a developed political theory. Saint-Just had a more systematic

cast of mind, but he died—at the age of twenty-six—before he could present a full account of his views. But from the material we have examined, we can construct a fairly clear sketch of the transition from corrupt existing society to a utopian ideal.

In both thinkers we see a combination of positive and negative measures—additional instantiation of virtue and terror. Robespierre was deeply concerned with purging the ruling elements, to keep the levers of power pure. At the same time, while the Revolution was being fought, he wished to have his proposed mechanisms of public education and civic religion established to regenerate the people. There is a certain disconnect between the means Robespierre proposed and the loftiness of the goal he believed the Revolution should achieve. Once again, in his February 5 speech:

> We want in a word to fulfill the course of nature, to accomplish the destiny of mankind, to make good the promises of philosophy, to absolve Providence from the long reign of crime and tyranny. (*Oeuvres,* X, 352)

If we take such rhetoric seriously, it is not clear how so grand an end could be reached, unless we attribute to Robespierre a Manichaean faith that after a final purge an era of purity and social harmony would begin. Perhaps the mechanisms Robespierre proposes could have contributed to developing a Spartan element in France—but this falls short of accomplishing mankind's destiny.

Saint-Just, in comparison, is less optimistic about the Revolution's goal. Spartanization of France is more apparent with him. Moreover, the extensive role he envisions for banishment and capital punishment indicates that the battle for virtue is never entirely won. Even in the realized republic, the fight against corruption continues.

If we consider Robespierre's proposed reforms in remove from his impossibly lofty rhetoric, important goals along the lines of a renewed Sparta do not seem out of reach. Although his plans for national education were less ambitious than what he would have liked, if put into practice, they could conceivably have raised the level of public-spiritedness, a process that would also have been supported by civic religion. In other respects, however, one can question the appropriateness of implementing Spartan institutions in eighteenth-century France. The improbability of such a plan is more apparent with Saint-Just than with Robespierre, although to be fair to Saint-Just, his plans may strike us as more absurd than Robespierre's because they are described in more detail.

Aside from problems with the ends they sought to realize, Robespierre and Saint-Just did not present adequate accounts of the necessary means. Here, I believe, we must return to Machiavelli's contention that the reformer must concentrate all power in his hands. The monumental challenge of re-creating the people required the same degree of unity and decisiveness as had been required to defeat the Revolution's enemies, which had made dictatorial government of the Committee of Public Safety necessary. It is understandable that Robespierre and Saint-Just focused their attention on the existing political situation and working within it. But again, there is a disconnect here: their power was not enough. This claim is based on more than the fact of their overthrow; they could not possibly have succeeded. Perhaps one reason for the suspicion that Robespierre wished to become a dictator was realization that the lofty ends of which he spoke were not possible without dictatorial power.

As we have seen, Robespierre's account of revolutionary government is an impressive extension of Montesquieu's analysis of the republic and the virtue required for its operation. But the revolutionary government Robespierre described was adequate only to defeat the Republic's enemies, not to establish a new order of things. Robespierre's proposals on civic education and religion were aimed at regeneration, the creation of a new people. But although these aspects of Robespierre's thought indicate clear realization of the need to shape new citizens, the means proposed could not be adequate unless supported by unified, dictatorial power. The institutions described by Saint-Just—shorn of their more extravagant features—could perhaps be effective in molding souls. But Saint-Just's *Institutions* is not accompanied by an account of how to put them into practice. It is possible that Saint-Just believed the Convention would vote to implement them. But that it actually ever would have done so strains credulity.

A great strength of Robespierre's theory of revolutionary government is that it addresses the question of moving forward from existing circumstances. The essence of his theory is the need to postpone implementing the legal and political niceties of an established republic in order to defeat the enemies who stand in the way of establishing it. The result is terror, which is justice swiftly applied. The Manuels describe Robespierre and Saint-Just as pioneers of the idea "of terror as the necessary path to utopia."[46] But beyond attacking identified enemies, it is not clear what this can accomplish. As Saint-Just says: "Terror is able to overthrow the monarch and aristocracy, but what will deliver us from corruption?" Once again, the answer: "Institutions" (*Oeuvres,* p. 976). Thus it is crucial to know how the institutions are to be established. But beyond terror, Robespierre and Saint-Just do not provide answers.

As developed in Robespierre's theory of revolutionary government, the use of terror was justified by circumstances. The extraordinary powers of the Committee of Public Safety were required to deal with emergency conditions, both foreign and domestic. In the spring of 1794, when the emergencies had been substantially overcome, the need to return to more ordinary government and to dismantle the Terror was widely felt. It is here that Robespierre's lack of power became apparent. Without clear enemies to target, the unity of the governing committees could not be maintained. The 22d Prairial law can be interpreted as an attempt to intensify the Terror in order to achieve other ends. But these goals were not clearly conceived or generally agreed on. The governing committees did not stand behind them, and there was not strong public support for them.

In large part the failure of Robespierre's theory must be attributed to the intangible quality of the goals he pursued. To return to points made at the beginning of this chapter, a Jacobin theory requires strong agreement among a small group of individuals (J.2; above, p. 92). In a large country such as France, this small group must swell to many thousands, or tens of thousands. But while these persons were strongly motivated by what they were against — the monarchy and aristocracy, the counterrevolution both abroad and at home — there was less agreement on what they were for. Regardless of the extent to which Robespierre's invocation of a vast conspiracy against the Revolution can be attributed to Machiavellian motives in addition to his paranoia, the existence of such a conspiracy fulfilled an important practical function: it provided a specific enemy around opposition to which friends of the Revolution could rally. "I know only two parties," Robespierre said in his last speech, "the party of good citizens and the party of the bad" (*Oeuvres,* X, 551). If this description had corresponded to reality, the way could have been clear: a final purge after which only good citizens remained. But of course reality was not so simple. After the Revolution's foes were eliminated, there was still the need for a tangible basis for unity among its friends.

Robespierre's power in the Convention and the Committee of Public Safety rested to a considerable degree on his close ties with the Parisian masses. But these too could not easily be translated into support for his ideal aspirations. To generate widespread support among the *sans-culottes,* Robespierre would have had to place their economic demands rather than the republic of virtue at the center of his program. Similarly, neither within nor outside the Committee of Public Safety or the Convention was there general support for his specific Rousseauian-Lycurgean goals.

In his speeches Robespierre shows clear awareness of questions of power in regard to its possible misuse. Because of the revolutionary government's extraordinary power, it requires extraordinary vigilance. Its mechanisms must be touched only by clean hands. "[T]he characteristic of popular government is confidence in the people and severity against itself" (*Oeuvres,* X, 356). We also note that this justified purging the government itself. But without an identifiable enemy, increased terror was a general threat and had to be stopped.

If Machiavelli's thesis about the need for concentrated power is true, then this would have had to be realized if Robespierre or Saint-Just was to succeed. There is, however, an obvious obverse side to Machiavelli's contention, which is recognized in his paradox concerning the need for an evil man to secure such power but a good one to use it properly. After the horrors of the past century, the dangers of concentrating complete power in single hands are too well known to require discussion. In ancient political theory, it was a trope that tyranny is potentially the best form of government, given the tyrant's power to do good, but also potentially the worst, for fear of the opposite. Although a tyrant's authority is necessary to establish the ideal republic, it also has the potential to subvert it entirely. Robespierre was aware of the need to prevent this. He insisted that power be reserved for clean hands. But what guarantee could he provide? Only virtue:

Virtue? It is a natural passion, without doubt. . . . [But] it exists, this tender, imperious, irresistible passion, the torment and the delight of magnanimous hearts; this profound horror of tyranny, this compassionate zeal for the oppressed, this sacred love of the fatherland, this purer and more holy love of humanity, without which a great revolution is only a crime, stirred up to destroy another crime; it exists, this generous ambition to found on earth the first Republic of the world; this self-assertion of free men who find a heavenly pleasure in the calm of a clear conscience and in the ravishing vision of public happiness. You feel it now burning in your souls; I feel it burning in mine. (*Oeuvres*, X, 554)

But then again, even if virtue is an adequate safeguard, how can it be recognized? I have noted that Robespierre followed Montesquieu and Rousseau in understanding virtue as subordination of one's private interest to the public interest. For his own virtue, Robespierre offered irrefutable proof, his willingness to sacrifice himself entirely: "How can one reproach a man who has truth on his side and who knows how to die for his country?" (X, 576). "O sublime people! Receive the sacrifice of all my being; happy is he who is born in your midst! Still happier he who can die for your happiness" (X, 445).

Robespierre was accused of attempting to become a dictator, a charge he vigorously resisted, although the realization of his ideals required one. But with all power concentrated in the hands of a unified dictatorship, there could be no means to ensure that those hands did not become impure.

CHAPTER SIX

The Marxian Alternative

Having reviewed a series of implementation theories encountered in the history of political theory, I turn to what is arguably the most influential, found in the works of Karl Marx and Friedrich Engels. We will look at the views of Marx and Engels themselves—frequently referred to below as views of Marx *simpliciter,* under the assumption that for the most part Engels was in agreement with Marx on the issues that interest us. Marx's views were developed in opposition to those of other political thinkers. I examine the so-called utopian socialist, Charles Fourier, and see how, in contrast to utopian socialism, Marxian socialism merits the designation "scientific." The following chapter will trace the anarchist reaction to Marx's dictatorship of the proletariat and then the development of Marx's view into the full-fledged Jacobinism of Lenin.

MARX'S THEORY OF REVOLUTION

Marx's theory of revolution is bound up with his views on historical materialism, class struggle, ideology, and the unity of theory and practice. Obviously, I cannot discuss all these aspects of Marx's system in detail. What most interests me are the central elements of Marx's theory of radical reform and how these relate to those of other radical political theorists during his period, especially the "utopian socialists" and the revolutionary anarchist, Mikhail Bakunin.

Marx is of course a theorist of proletarian revolution. Central to his theory is the gradual development of class consciousness among the proletariat and their transformation from separate individuals into a class, in which the grievances of individual members come to be recognized as class grievances, common to the members of the class, and they are led by this increased awareness to struggle against their bourgeois oppressors. In accordance with historical materialism, Marx sees this happening as a result of the proletariat's deteriorating economic situation. Driven to take action by their increasingly dire circumstances, proletarians provoke retaliatory action from the bourgeoisie. This causes their own awareness to increase, causing them to resist ever more, thereby provoking increased retaliation, and so increased resistance, in an intensifying spiral of action and counteraction. Central to Marx's view of the "unity of theory and practice" is the belief that revolutionary consciousness and revolutionary activity develop in reciprocal interaction, eventually culminating in revolution against the oppressing class.

Marx's belief in the unity of theory and practice commits him to the view that possibilities for political change are always determined by existing circumstances. Although Marx and Engels believe that the discovery of new, theoretical ideas is a necessary part of moving to a new society, these ideas are not discovered by an individual man of genius. Rather, they grow out of a historical situation that makes the relevant changes possible. This is not to say individual men of genius do not arise and propagate ideas with far-reaching consequences. However, if the times are not ripe for the *proper reception* of their ideas, they will fall on deaf ears and have little influence. For example, ideas strikingly similar to Luther's were propagated earlier by a series of religious reformers, notably Wycliff, in England, and Hus, in Bohemia. But because times were not ripe, these figures were not successful. The reason Luther succeeded was not because of the superior quality of his ideas but because the times were right to receive them. According to Engels, something similar would have been true of Marx's own ideas. Because the time was ripe, if Marx had not developed his theory, another thinker would have come along and done so. Ideas along those lines were in the air.[1]

Marx believes that one necessary condition for the successful reception of revolutionary ideas is the existence of a class able to receive them. Revolutionary ideas will blossom when they express the objective interests of class members. The economic and social circumstances of the class are thus primary; ideas that express these are secondary. But ideas are nevertheless important. According to Marx, a class is more than a group of people with similar interests. Unless members of the group become aware of their interests, they remain a class "in itself," only potentially a class; they become an actual class, a class "for itself," when they become aware of their interests and so begin to struggle with other classes in order to realize them. This has the effect of further increasing their struggle, and so their consciousness, and so on. But still, the active expression of revolutionary ideas presupposes circumstances in which they can have real effects and so the existence of a revolutionary class.

Marx's understanding of his theory and his activity as a theorist should be interpreted in this context. Theorists play an essential role in helping a class to articulate its interests. Marx believes his theory is superior to other socialist theories because it more accurately expresses the class interests of the rising proletariat. Only insofar as it corresponds to the interests of this class can his theory be effective, and its effectiveness is limited by the obduracy of existing circumstances. Nevertheless, the expression of theoretical ideas can make a difference. As Marx writes in *Capital,* a society "can neither clear by bold leaps, nor remove by legal enactments, the obstacles offered by the successive phases of its normal development. But it can shorten and lessen the birth-pangs."[2] Societies follow an objectively determined course of development. But within these parameters, the articulation of proper ideas can speed up the process of transition from one stage to the next.

Revolutionary ideas can facilitate the movement between historical stages if they accurately reflect the interests of the rising class. Because the theory in question should express conclusions to which members of the class are being driven by the circumstances of their lives, the standard for assessing revolutionary ideas is whether or not they are adopted by the revolutionary class. In the case of Marx's ideas, the standard is whether they represent the proletariat's needs and so are discoveries members of this class are making themselves because of the harshness of their lives. Marx and Engels describe the important relationship between communist ideas and the circumstances of the revolutionary class in the *Communist Manifesto:*

> The theoretical conclusions of the Communists are in no way based on ideas or principles that have been invented, or discovered, by this or that would-be universal reformer.
>
> They merely express, in general terms, actual relations springing from an existing class struggle, from a historical movement going on under our very eyes. (*Works,* I, 120)

Revolutionary ideas must be adopted by the class whose interests they express. Because Marx believes they cannot be *imposed* on the class, he is an apostle of essentially spontaneous revolution. The proletariat will act in concert to bring about revolutionary change, because it is being driven to take this action by its actual circumstances. As its condition deteriorates, its members become aware of the faults of the existing order and the need for revolution. This pattern is in contrast to one in which the proletariat is *led* to espouse revolutionary ideas by an organization of revolutionary ideologues or a vanguard party. Marx classically expresses the idea that the workers must make their own revolution in the "General Rules of the International Working Men's Association": "the emancipation of the working classes must be conquered by the working classes themselves" (*Works,* II, 19).[3]

The idea of spontaneous revolution does not prevent a revolutionary party from playing a significant role. Its role, however, must be secondary to the developing consciousness of class members brought about by their material conditions. A classic expression of the party's role is given in the *Communist Manifesto:*

> Finally, in times when the class struggle nears the decisive hour, the process of dissolution going on within the ruling class, in fact within the whole range of old society, assumes such a violent, glaring char-

acter, that a small section of the ruling class cuts itself adrift, and joins the revolutionary class, the class that holds the future in its hands. Just as, therefore, at an earlier period, a section of the nobility went over to the bourgeoisie, so now a portion of the bourgeoisie goes over to the proletariat, and in particular, a portion of the bourgeois ideologists, who have raised themselves to the level of comprehending theoretically the historical movement as a whole. (*Works,* I, 117)

When circumstances are reaching a climax, the propagation of revolutionary ideas can help the rising class to achieve full awareness and so take necessary action. As happened during the French Revolution, the necessary ideologists will be from the ruling class—as is the case with Marx and Engels themselves, both members of the bourgeoisie. The proletariat's need for bourgeois ideologists is clear, in that members of this class do not have the education necessary to develop a theoretically sophisticated account of present and future conditions. But regardless of their philosophical power, a group of ideologists can contribute to the growing consciousness of the revolutionary class only if their theories are closely related to conclusions the class is spontaneously coming to of its own accord.

Marx's view of the unity of theory and practice places him at odds with other theorists, who believed that correct theory must precede practice, with the latter intended to realize the former. Many of the thinkers discussed in the previous chapters had moral ideals that they wished to bring into existence. Marx differs from these theorists in seeing revolutionary consciousness and revolutionary action developing cojointly. Important opponents of Marx held the more traditional opinion that theory came first. Prominent exponents of this position were utopian socialists and Blanquists. The latter were radical groups that took their name from Louis-Auguste Blanqui (1805–81), a French socialist, who advocated achieving socialism through conspiratorial political activity.[4] Marx's relationship to the Blanquists is discussed below. I turn now to the view of Charles Fourier, a representative utopian socialist. After examining his ideas on the ideal future society and how to get there, I explore Marx's criticisms of utopian socialism, which further sharpens the distinctive features of Marx's view.

THE NEWTON OF THE SOCIAL WORLD

A view on realizing the ideal society that is virtually the opposite of educational realism is presented by Charles Fourier. Rather than remake men as the basis of improved society, Fourier's goal is to remake society to fit men's true nature, which, once so liberated, will shine forth in almost divine glory.

Fourier was born at Besançon, France, in 1772 and lived an outwardly uneventful life. He published his first major works, *Theory of the Four Movements* and *Social Destiny of Man,* while employed as a commercial traveler for textile firms. An inheritance he received in 1812 allowed him to devote his full efforts to theorizing and attempts to put his ideas into practice—with some though not striking success.

To a large extent Fourier is a figure of ridicule in the history of political thought. His theory combines the outlandish and the brilliant, inextricably bound. As George Lichtheim says, "He is almost *too* interesting."[5] Some of his ideas are utterly ridiculous, for example, transformation of the seas into lemonade, people developing additional eyes in the backs of their heads so that they can see behind them, and transformation of animal pests into so-called antibeasts. But for reasons we will see, throughout his writings the profoundly serious and profoundly silly often cannot be disentangled.

Fourier's theory is composed of two interwoven strands, a critique of "civilization"—which for him is a term of opprobrium—and an alternative organization of society. These two strands can be presented in turn. Fourier despised bourgeois society and excoriated both commerce and bourgeois morality—work and love. He noted the terrible abuses caused by the market economy. These included poverty, the horrors of woman and child labor, and sanctification of private property, which permitted its holders to destroy crops and cause starvation, in order to raise prices and profits.

Throughout his life Fourier had a mania for enumeration and classification. This was evident by the age of five, when he feared he had committed all sins recognized by the Catholic Church.[6] Fourier classified the seven vices of commerce: bankruptcy, usury, speculation, hoarding, cheating, parasitism, and smuggling. Each of these was in turn broken down into subvices; for instance, Fourier noted three orders, nine types, and thirty-six species of bankruptcy.[7] Blistering criticism was directed at all four bases of commercial society: production, consumption, distribution, and circulation. For instance, in regard to production, Fourier attacked the inefficiency engendered by the duplication of function that resulted from many small farms and factories instead of fewer large ones. He listed twelve classes of people he considered unproductive idlers and went on to criticize the fact that many workers were denied the right to work, and when they did find work, it was performed in loathsome conditions. Fourier came to believe that work was not necessarily dehumanizing. It became so only when workers were forced to labor for up to fifteen hours a day in filthy surroundings.

Fourier's critique of civilization exists on two levels. In addition to his account of the readily discernible abuses and miseries of bourgeois society is his analysis of psychological suffering. Anticipating the views of Nietzsche and Freud, Fourier's system is based on a developed theory of repression and the damage it causes. The alternative he proposes is meant to solve the problems of civilization on both immediate and psychological levels.

Fourier's alternative to civilization is discovered through a new science, based on "Passionate Attraction." In the same sense that God has provided a consistent mechanism for ordering the physical world, gravitation, he must have provided a mechanism for ordering the social world. The task is to find this second principle, and, of course, Fourier believed that he had found it—attraction. He thought he had discovered the key to the ordering of the social world, the passions, in the same sense that Newton had discovered gravitation.

The passions inherent in man's nature are the work of God. By giving them free rein, a new social order can be established and all society's problems overcome. Like the gods of Olympus, the Apostles, and the signs of the Zodiac, the passions are twelve in number. They fall into three groups. The five "luxurious passions" are the five senses. The four "appetites of the soul" are friendship, love, ambition, and paternity. The last group, Fourier's own discovery, are the three "distributive passions," "cabaliste," "papillonne" or butterfly, and "composite." Cabaliste is a passion for intrigue in groups, papillonne is a passion for variety, and composite is a passion for pleasures that involve both the body and the mind simultaneously.

Fourier believed that these passions are absolute and immutable: "[T]he twelve passions are eternal, unalterable, like the three principles of nature from which they derive. I do not possess, God that I am, the ability to alter them."[8] Hence nature is not to be denied; the concept of repression is basic to Fourier's system:

> Passion stifled at one point breaks out at another, like waters blocked by a dike; it reverberates like the fluid of a prematurely closed ulcer.[9]

> If you chase nature out the door, she comes in by the window. (*UV*, p. 304)

All the miseries of civilization are caused by various forms of the denial and repression of the passions. In Fourier's new society, Harmony, all the passions will be unleashed. A superstructure of social relationships will be constructed on the substructural network of natural, passional relationships, and all social problems will melt into the air.

Reorganized Society

Liberation of the passions will afford humankind delights heretofore unimagined. The basic structure of Fourier's thought is simple, although his alternative society—the "phalanstery" or "phalanx"—is remarkably complex. The Manuels explain in part how it came to be so complex:

> Fourier had an excellent memory, which he nourished with an endless supply of facts seemingly gathered at random. Once the Idea of the phalanstery had taken shape, every chance bit of information was assimilated into the infinitely detailed and complicated system of living and working arrangements which he projected. Fourier was constantly collecting, counting, cataloguing and analyzing. If he took a walk in Paris and a small hotel appealed to him, its proportions

became the basis for the architectural framework of a phalanstery building.[10]

Fourier's ideal society is organized in small communities, each composed of between 1,600 and 1,800 members. The phalanstery resembles a large hotel—although owned by the guests—in that all the members live together in an enormous central building that also houses the community's few factories. The size of the community is determined by Fourier's enumeration of all the possible personality types, classified according to the distribution of passions. He believed there were 810 distinct types; if the phalanstery were to have one of each sex, then membership would be 1,620. The ideal phalanstery would be an arena for the clash of different personality types. The contrasts and conflicts in the members' passional makeups would complement each other and contribute to the well-being of all involved.

The phalanstery is organized according to the passional makeup of individuals. The basic organizational unit is the passionate series, which is a network of groups, each of which is animated by some nuance or variety of a particular passion. A passionate series is always composed of groups, never individuals, and the members of each group cooperate harmoniously in the pursuit of their common passion while competing with the other groups in the series, which are motivated by related but different passions. For example, in the pear growers series, the white pear group would compete with the yellow pear group and the brown pear group and so on, each group animated by a passion for its particular kind of pear.

The passionate series underlies Fourier's revolutionary ideas concerning making work pleasant. In Harmony the passionate series are meshed. An individual will be a member of at least thirty groups. The phalanstery's economy is based on agriculture (horticulture actually). In Harmony people labor out of the desire to labor, not to satisfy physical needs, and the three distributive passions guarantee that work will be a source of pleasure. Papillonne, the passion for variety, is satisfied by ensuring a rotation of functions. Nobody works at any one job for more than two hours, and less desirable jobs are rotated every hour. The labor itself is done by groups, thereby unleashing the cabaliste passion for intrigue.

The members of contiguous groups will cooperate in a fierce rivalry with the other groups of their series. Because the work itself will be done in pleasant surroundings, the composite passion will also be satisfied. The fulfilling labor of the phalanstery will be a source of never-ending joy; the day will not be long enough for all the pleasant, challenging jobs in which the residents of Harmony wish to engage.

Fourier can be criticized for not foreseeing the importance of industrialization and its implications. One reason for this is his observation that factory labor is less attractive than work in the fields. Because he saw labor as attractive, not repulsive, unlike Marx, he was not interested in cutting the working day. In Harmony the realm of freedom does not lie beyond necessity; to a large extent freedom consists of the enjoyment of attractive labor, which, although attractive, is still necessary for the subsistence of the community. But in another sense, in assuring each member of society a minimum even if he does not work, Fourier, like Marx, placed the realm of freedom for the individual beyond necessity.

In Harmony production will increase, and the plague of scarcity will become a thing of the past. Even the least desirable jobs will be made attractive. Degrading jobs, as well as lasting no more than an hour, will be afforded social prestige. Disgusting jobs will allow young boys to exercise their penchant for filth, organized in "Little Hordes." More taxing, large-scale work projects will be undertaken by industrial armies, organized from the members of neighboring phalansteries. Spurred on by sexual and other inducements, these armies will complete major projects and be able to work such miracles as greening the deserts through enormous concentrations of labor power.

Fourier's solutions to problems of love and sexuality are similarly striking. In Harmony free love will reign. There will be no guilt, no repression. As well as ensuring each member an economic minimum, Fourier guarantees every individual a sexual minimum. Once lust is satiated, sentimental love can reign supreme. Matching services will be established to ensure the gratification of every member of society, no matter how peculiar his sexual appetites. Fourier's system of free love—as revealed in *Le nouveau monde amoureux,* unpublished until 1967[11]—provides endless, tedious detail concerning Vestals and Damsels, provisions for travelers, Angelic Couples, and a minutiae of regulations. As critics are quick to point out, this lonely, prissy bachelor must have spent countless hours enumerating the delights of the world to come.

Because unleashing the passions will create happiness and harmony, Fourier's utopia is anarchistic. Men will not have to be forced to work but will do so of their own accord, and they will love each other genuinely and spontaneously. The harmonious interaction of individuals explains Fourier's political theory; for all intents and purposes, he has none. The need for coercion will vanish with the other ills of civilization.

Destructive passions will be channeled in healthy directions. Even Nero, a man with bloodthirsty inclinations, will become a constructive citizen, by becoming a butcher and so channeling his aggression (*UV*, pp. 303–7). Ordinary aggressive tendencies will be channeled through the fierce competition of the groups in every passionate series. As for problems such as jealousy, they will be lessened greatly through the operation of the sexual minimum. Fourier discerned the fact that jealousy, in the destructive form it takes in bourgeois society, is a result of frustration and repression. By eliminating such dissatisfaction, Harmony can eliminate the evils of human nature (*UV*, pp. 336–46). Free from the moral constraints of existing society, secure in the guarantee of both an economic and a sexual minimum, the fortunate beings of Harmony will live lives of unending delights.

IMPLEMENTING THE IDEAL STATE

Other aspects of Fourier's system could be discussed. But what we have seen should suffice for understanding his governing ideas. His central insight, pursued relentlessly throughout the phalanstery's complex details, is that through unleashing man's passionate nature, true happiness can be attained. Fourier is far removed from Freud, who sees a tragic conflict between man's instinctual nature and the demands of civilization. If throughout history civilization has been loathsome, has degraded men, and made them miserable, this is because the right kind of civilization has not been tried. To move to a superior society, we must do only two things: (a) find the immutable laws that are meant to order the social world; and (b) reconstruct society in accordance with them:

In answer to criticism upon his theory, Fourier was accustomed to say: "There are but two points to be determined; first whether I have really discovered these Laws; and second, whether I have made a correct deduction from them. If I have failed in either of these particulars, let men of science point out my errors and execute the work which I have undertaken. Let them discover the Laws and make the deductions."[12]

Once the laws of passionate attraction have been derived, the second step is to deduce a social system that will allow them free rein, as in the phalanstery.

But even if Fourier is correct about man's passional makeup, he still confronts the problem of moving to the superior society. He believes that the only way he can prove the validity of his system is to implement it and demonstrate conclusively that it works. Because of the complexity of human passions, the system must be realized in its entirety, with all 810 passionate types represented. Fourier's hope is that once a single phalanstery is established, the rest of the human race will see the enormous profits and pleasures it affords. They will spontaneously organize more and more similar communities, until the entire globe is composed of an interlocking series of phalansteries, existing in peace and harmony.

Accordingly, Fourier spent his adult life trying to find a backer. He appealed to politicians, noblemen, and wealthy capitalists. He returned to his room each day at noon and waited for the expected benefactor to arrive, but no one came.

To a large extent Fourier wrote his works to attract the necessary backers. Thus the works cannot be taken at face value. As the Manuels say, he was a forerunner of the "great advertising heroes."[13] Commentators note the chaotic presentation of Fourier's works. According to Charles Gide:

All these volumes bear, indeed, a strong resemblance to each other, especially as each contains the author's entire system, and exhibits, pell-mell, the same theories, reproduced for the most part, in about the same terms; whoever has read one of them, particularly the "Association Domestique Agricole," has read them all.[14]

There was a method to Fourier's *ordre dispersée*. He crammed every book with never-ending descriptions of the delights of the new amorous world, sexual and financial, parades and lemonade, imaginary and otherwise, and the tremendous honors that would be the reward of the wealthy aristocrat or politician who first showed the courage to defy opinion and implement the system. It seems that Fourier would have said anything, written anything to induce someone to put up the money for a trial phalanx, and his books reflect this. In Fourier's defense, one should recognize that the books themselves meant relatively little to him, although he scrupulously included the complete framework of the new social order in each one, in case a potential backer read only one. The books were a means toward an end. Fourier knew that the system would work and published his works in order to attract someone who would implement it.

Toward the end of his life, Fourier's desire to change the world achieved a measure of success. He attracted disciples, and a movement was begun in his name. Fourierist model societies began to be erected.[15] The first was in Romania, where a noble landowner experimented with the system among his serfs. But surrounding landowners, fearing the spread of such dangerous practices, invaded and destroyed the new society. In Russia Mikhail Vasilevich Petrashevsky, a revolutionary of 1848, attempted to implement the system among the peasants on his estate. But his house was burned to the ground. The most famous follower of Petrashevsky's Fourierism was Fyodor Dostoyevsky, who was arrested and placed before a firing squad, in 1849, for revolutionary ideas. In the United States, in the 1840s and 1850s, some thirty phalansteries were founded, the most famous of which was the model community at Brook Farm. But all these failed because of internal conflicts or financial difficulties.[16] As the Manuels say, a "complete history of Fourierism and its influence would have to cover much territory, settlements ranging from the prairies of mid-nineteenth century America to the kibbutzim of modern Israel." But none of these attempts conformed closely to Fourier's plan. None had all the requisite personality types, or liberated all repressed passion. To quote the Manuels once again: "One thing is certain, the Master would have rejected each and every one of [these attempts] as vicious falsifications of the doctrine."[17]

As a utopian, Fourier can be viewed in a basic sense as the opposite of Plato. I have discussed educational realism and Plato's single-minded attempt to use all the resources of the state to impose virtue on its citizens. Although plans for education were an important aspect of Fourier's system (though not discussed above), this is intended not to restrain the passions but to liberate them. Rather than shape men according to a divinely ordained conception of virtue, Fourier believed in shaping society according to the divinely ordained allotment of the passions. Man is not molded to fit society but society to fit man. In a letter to his disciple, Victor Considerant, Fourier wrote: "I am the only reformer who has rallied round human nature by accepting it as it is and devising the means of utilizing it with all the defects which are inseparable from man."[18]

A society of this kind, based on liberation of the passions, does not rest well with coercive means to establish it, and Fourier did not seriously consider such means.[19] Like Socrates, he relied on persuasion, but again with a different spin. Enticement was central to Fourier's persuasive endeavor. In the *Gorgias* Plato compares competition between a philosopher and a rhetor before a crowd of their fellow citizens to a contest between a doctor and a pastry cook before a jury of children (464d–65a). Plato's purpose, of course, is to denounce the rhetor as a panderer. But the role Fourier occupied was that of the pastry cook.

Socrates believed that virtue implied happiness, and so that in espousing his conception of virtue, he was appealing to what people truly desired. But the conception of happiness he expounded did not coincide with people's conscious desires. Socratic virtue is a hard road, never pursued by the many. For Fourier, the road is the opposite, and he appealed to what Socrates would regard as man's baser instincts. The phalanstery promises never-ending joy because of its ability to satisfy these instincts. Throughout his life Fourier could not understand why people were not attracted to his ideas. He wrote and cajoled and waited for lightning to strike. But in spite of the phalanstery's delights, the dead hand of existing society stifled interest in ideas so novel.

SCIENTIFIC SOCIALISM

Having reviewed the main elements of Fourier's view, I return to Marx. Marx believed his theory was distinctive in being "scientific socialism." Like other theorists he examined and criticized, Marx had a vision of a better society and was interested in doing whatever possible to bring it about. But he believed his theory was superior to others in two important respects: (a) in regard to the nature of the goal he sought to attain; and (b) in regard to the means for bringing this about. In addition to Fourier, the *Communist Manifesto* identifies Robert Owen and Henri de Saint-Simon as utopian socialists. According to Marx, what characterized these figures is the fact that they *drew up* plans for the future society and then set about ascertaining how to make their ideas real. Not having access to the requisite means of coercion, they attempted to *persuade* people to put their ideas into practice. I have discussed the extent to which Fourier succeeded in his aims, while given what we have seen in previous chapters, his lack of success is not surprising.

Marx criticized the utopian socialists for overreliance on reason, and this in two senses. In contrast to his belief that revolution would be based on the developing class consciousness of the proletariat, the utopian socialists sought to revolutionize society through the power of their reason alone. They used reason to derive their plans for future society; and then, having no other means to bring these ends about, they relied on the power of reason to compel assent. Marx believed that utopian socialists had to take this path because they were hampered by the times during which they wrote. Because their times were not yet open to revolution, they were forced to look elsewhere. A classic criticism along these lines is found in the *Communist Manifesto:*

> Since the development of class antagonism keeps even pace with the development of industry, the economic situation, as they find it, does not as yet offer to them the material conditions for the emancipation of the proletariat. They therefore search after a new social science, after new social laws, that are to create these conditions.
>
> Historical action is to yield to their personal inventive action, historically created conditions of emancipation to fantastic ones, and

the gradual spontaneous class-organization of the proletariat to the organization of society specially contrived by these inventors. Future history resolves itself, in their eyes, into the propaganda and the practical carrying out of their social plans. (*Works,* I, 134)

Believing in the force of their ideas, the utopian socialists did not pursue political means:

Hence, they reject all political, and especially all revolutionary action; they wish to attain their ends by peaceful means, and endeavor, by small experiments, necessarily doomed to failure, and by the force of example, to pave the way for the new social Gospel. (*Works,* I, 135)

For how can people, when once they understand their system, fail to see in it the best possible plan of the best possible state of society? (*Works,* I, 135)

Because the science of the new society is valid at all times, under all conditions, its implementation can occur at any time. It does not depend on historical forces; the only necessary condition is the discovery of the new social science by an individual prophetic figure and his ability to compel widespread assent through the force of his reason. In Engels's words, in *Socialism: Utopian and Scientific:*

If pure reason and justice have not, hitherto, ruled the world, this has been the case only because men have not rightly understood them. What was wanted was the individual man of genius, who has now arisen and who understands the truth. That he has now arisen, that the truth has now been clearly understood, is not an inevitable event, following of necessity in the chain of historical development, but a mere happy accident. He might just as well have been born 500 years earlier, and might then have spared humanity 500 years of error, strife, and suffering. (*Works,* III, 117)

As "scientific socialism," Marx's theory is distinct from other forms of socialism in not being a *theory* but an expression of the revolutionary class-consciousness of the rising proletariat. In Marx's eyes, this class has before it a radical historical mission. As it develops consciousness of its situation, the proletariat will act to relieve its plight, thereby bringing the new order into existence. Marx's account of future society is not a "theory" but a description of the historical forces leading the proletariat to understand its condition. The details of future society will be worked out by historical forces. Marx does not have in mind a blueprint; as he says in *Capital,* he will not write recipes for the cookshops of the future (I, 17). The shape of the future will emerge through the developing class consciousness of the proletariat. And because the proletariat's developing consciousness impels it in this direction, Marx does not have to rely on the force of his reason to persuade them to act. They are driven to do so by their historical circumstances. Accordingly, in an introduction he wrote to Marx's *Class Struggles in France,* in 1895, Engels describes the ideas that will win over the proletariat as "ideas which were the truest reflection of their economic condition, which were nothing but the clear, rational expression of their needs, of needs not yet understood but merely vaguely felt by them" (*Works,* I, 191). In *Civil War in France,* Marx writes:

> The [working class] have no ready-made utopias to introduce *par décret du peuple* [by decree of the people]. They know that in order to work out their own emancipation, and along with it that higher form to which present society is irresistibly tending by its own economical agencies, they will have to pass through long struggles, through a series of historic processes, transforming circumstances and men. They have no ideals to realize, but to set free the elements of the new society with which collapsing bourgeois society itself is pregnant. (*Works,* II, 224)

In *Socialism: Utopian and Scientific,* Engels says of the clash between the productive forces and class structure in capitalist society: "Modern socialism is nothing but the reflex, in thought, of this conflict in fact; its ideal reflection in the minds, first, of the class directly suffering under it, the working class" (*Works,* III, 134–35).

Because the rising consciousness of the proletariat depends on economic conditions that are beyond people's immediate power to bring about, the revolutionary party must play a secondary role. This is one respect in which Marx's own thought diverges sharply from Marxism-Leninism, which places enormous weight on the Party and its tasks. In the *Communist Manifesto,* Marx argues that the revolutionary party must be closely connected with the revolutionary class:

> The Communists do not form a separate party opposed to other working-class parties.
>
> They have no interests separate and apart from those of the proletariat as a whole.
>
> They do not set up any sectarian principles of their own, by which to shape and mold the proletarian movement. (*Works,* I, 119)

The major respect in which the party stands above the class is in its superior understanding of the latter's interests. But this merely constitutes understanding the direction in which the proletariat as a whole will necessarily develop (*Works,* I, 484).

MARXISM AND BLANQUISM

Thus we see that, in contrast to the utopian socialists, Marx does not believe in a predetermined, correct revolutionary theory or blueprint for the new society, which political activity is to realize. Rather, proper theory emerges from political activity in the interactive form discussed above. Given his view that ideas follow on material circumstances, Marx would doubtless reject the idea that, even if it could be discovered, a true revolutionary ideal could be achieved through the force of persuasion. Unless the ideal in question corresponded closely to the consciousness of the potentially revolutionary class, they would not accept it. But this still leaves open the possibility that true ideas could be achieved through force.

During his long political career, Marx at times flirted with the idea of forcible imposition of his revolutionary ideas on society as a whole. Most notable was his membership in the Communist League, on behalf of which he and Engels wrote the *Communist Manifesto.* The League was heavily influenced by the ideas of Blanqui, who as noted above was a French socialist, who believed in the realization of socialism through conspiratorial political activity.

In an 1874 criticism of the Blanquists, Engels described their program as follows:

> Since Blanqui regards every revolution as a coup de main of a small revolutionary minority, it automatically follows that its success must inevitably be followed by the establishment of a dictatorship—not it should be well noted, of the entire revolutionary class, the proletariat, but of the small number of those who accomplished the insurrection and who themselves are at first organised under the dictatorship of one or several persons. (*Works*, III, 381)

Marx's association with Blanquist groups cannot be discussed in detail here. It should be sufficient to note that, like the Jacobins, extreme Blanquists argued that the purpose of the postrevolutionary dictatorship was to educate the masses. Although during the late 1840s Marx was associated with Blanquist organizations, it is important to recognize that he never subscribed to their ideas.[20] Criticizing Blanquist organizations, in 1850 Marx wrote:

> It goes without saying that these conspirators do not restrict themselves simply to organizing the revolutionary proletariat. Their business consists precisely in forestalling the process of revolutionary development, spurring it into artificial crises, making revolutions extempore without the conditions of revolution. For them the only condition required for revolution is the sufficient organization of their own conspiracy. They are the alchemists of revolution, and they share in every way the deranged notions and narrow-minded fixed ideas of the alchemists of old. They grasp eagerly at new contraptions to achieve the revolutionary miracle: incendiary bombs, explosive devices with magical powers, and rioting that is supposed to have effects all the more wondrous and astonishing the less it has any rational basis. Busy with such plot-mongering, they have no further aim than the next assault on the existing regime and look with deepest

disdain upon a more theoretical enlightenment of the workers as to their class interests.[21]

Blanquists are like utopian socialists in overlooking the unity of theory and practice. According to Marx, once again, revolutionary ideas must wait on revolutionary conditions. They cannot be created by the propagation of universal truths, or through conspiratorial organizations that are able to seize political power. Should such a conspiracy succeed, this would merely inaugurate a period of political dictatorship rather than the desired socialism. Socialism requires the existence of necessary objective conditions, while the existence of these will be signaled by the organization of a class that is forced by its material interests to pursue a socialist program. Marx believed he lived in a privileged time, in that the emergence of the proletariat had made communism, which was otherwise impossible, not only possible but inevitable.

Accordingly, in all his works Marx never advocates having the party seize political power and then use this to educate the masses. If the proletariat achieves revolutionary consciousness, domination by an elite party is unnecessary. If the proletariat does not develop, elite domination is no substitute for objective conditions that make revolution possible. In his detailed study of Marx's and Engels's political thought through all stages of their development, R. N. Hunt concludes as follows:

> Perhaps the key distinguishing feature of Marx and Engels' thinking, among the diverse currents of early socialism, was precisely their conviction, their ultimate democratic faith, that the masses could and would educate *themselves,* organize *themselves,* liberate *themselves,* and rule *themselves.* No external agent, no *deus ex machina* in the form of an enlightened elite, was required in their vision, although of course they never denied the incidental helpfulness of intellectuals like themselves.[22]

Because of the predominant role of material conditions in shaping class consciousness, Marx believes the party's role is necessarily limited to helping to "shorten the birth-pangs" of the new society.

The Dictatorship of the Proletariat

Given his faith in a revolution that is basically spontaneous, Marx has relatively little to say about the details of the transition to communism. These, like other aspects of future society, will be worked out historically. But Marx believes in the need for a transitional political organization, a state controlled by the victorious proletariat. He refers to this as "the dictatorship of the proletariat." This is of course one of the most celebrated of Marx's ideas, referred to by Lenin as the "touchstone on which the *real* understanding and recognition of Marxism should be tested."[23] But Marx discusses it remarkably infrequently in his works. In his entire corpus, the idea of dictatorship is linked with the working class only some sixteen times, in eleven separate writings.[24] Only one of these, *Class Struggles in France,* can be considered a major work — and even this should be classified as journalism rather than a theoretical statement. Probably the idea's clearest expression is in the *Critique of the Gotha Program* (1875). Marx wrote this work in the form of a private letter to leaders of the German Socialist movement. It was published only after his death. Marx writes:

> Between capitalist and communist society lies the period of the revolutionary transformation of the one into the other. Corresponding to this is also a political transition period in which the state can be nothing but *the revolutionary dictatorship of the proletariat.* (*Works,* III, 26)

Though this notion is not found in Marx's major statements of his theory, it seems clear that he viewed it as an important part of his theory. This is seen in another famous passage, contained in a letter to Joseph Weydemeyer written in 1852:

> Insofar as I am concerned, the merit of having discovered either the existence of classes in modern society or the class struggle does not belong to me. Bourgeois historians have presented the historic development of this struggle of classes, and bourgeois economists the economic anatomy of the same, long before I did. What was new in what

> I did was: (1) to demonstrate that the *existence of classes* is tied only to *definite historical phases of development of production;* (2) that the class struggle necessarily leads to the *dictatorship of the proletariat;* (3) that this dictatorship is only a transition to the *dissolution of all classes* and leads to the formation of a *classless society.* (Marx to Joseph Weydemeyer, March 5, 1852; *Letters,* p. 81)

As these passages indicate, Marx believes in the necessity of a state during the period after the revolution, before the transformation to communist society is complete. This belief distinguishes Marx's view from those of anarchist thinkers — as we will see. The anarchists believed the state could be abolished immediately. Though Marx is not an anarchist in regard to means, the dictatorship of the proletariat is a transitional form, leading to an anarchistic end state. Communism, which will be a classless society, will also be without political institutions wielded by a ruling class to suppress other classes.

Marx does not say exactly what the dictatorship of the proletariat will do during the transitional period. It is likely that it will be exercised against recalcitrant elements of the bourgeoisie, who, having been overthrown, must still be reincorporated into the new society.[25] In the few contexts in which Marx explicitly discusses what this will do, its function is mainly forcibly suppressing the enemies of the working class. The dictatorship of the proletariat is the government of the proletariat over the remnants of the bourgeoisie, not a dictatorship of the party over the proletariat. Marx never conceives the dictatorship of the proletariat as a government of the minority who know over the majority who do not.

On the whole, too much should not be made of the dictatorship of the proletariat in Marx's works. At the time Marx wrote, the idea of dictatorship connoted a temporary period of emergency rule not bound by law, along the lines of what existed in the Roman republic. There is strong evidence that Marx believed that in countries with developed democratic systems, the proletariat could come to power peacefully and so that the dictatorship of the proletariat would be a democratic state under universal suffrage.[26] Once again, because Marx believes the revolution will be made by the class-conscious proletariat, there is no hint in his theory that a transitional period is required to allow a party of ideologues to employ state power in order to educate the masses. This idea, central to Jacobinism and Blanquism—and then, in the twentieth century, to Marxism-Leninism—is absent from Marx's thought.[27]

The Fate of the Revolution

To close out this account of Marx's views concerning the realization of his ideal end state, I present two criticisms. First, because he is a theorist of essentially spontaneous revolution, Marx is able to avoid important theoretical difficulties that plague other theorists. He does not have to rely on the force of logical arguments to transform society, as did the utopian socialists. Nor does he have to deal with problems inherent in seizure of power by a revolutionary band. His belief that historical forces will work things out eliminates the need for either of these courses. The proletariat is forced to rise because of material conditions. Organized political parties play a relatively small role in the process. Their primary contribution is helping the prerevolutionary proletariat develop class consciousness. Probably the greatest blow Marx's theory suffered was when things did not work out as he had foreseen. Capitalism turned out to be far more resilient than he had imagined. Throughout western Europe and North America, the past one hundred fifty years have witnessed tremendous economic growth. It is commonly said that Marx mistook the birth pangs of capitalism for its death throes. Throughout the history of capitalist society, there have been significant periods of economic panic and depression, with severe consequences for millions of people. But these have been the exception rather than the rule. The state has proved resilient as well, developing institutions to provide an essential economic and social safety net for virtually all citizens. The proletariat was transformed by these developments but not in the direction Marx anticipated. Politically enfranchised and relatively prosperous, the proletariat ceased to be a revolutionary force. That things were working out in this direction was apparent in western Europe by the end of the nineteenth century, and socialist parties generally moved in the direction of democratic reform. Within the Marxian tradition, these developments were clearly recognized by the "revisionist" theorist Eduard Bernstein, who was a close associate of Engels and an important figure in the German Social Democratic Party. Bernstein argued that Marx's major predictions were incorrect. On the basis of abundant empirical evidence, he contended that the working class was no longer revolutionary; its members wished to become middle class. Socialism, a political system in which their needs were addressed by the government, did not entail overthrowing the liberal order but *extending* it. According to Bernstein, extensive social welfare programs would be implemented by the state as the working class came increasingly to control it. To achieve socialism, the "liberal institutions of modern society . . . do not need to be destroyed; they need only to be further developed."[28]

Regardless of the details of Bernstein's analysis, there is little question that the overall course of events has confirmed his forecast. In 1895, looking back on the development of capitalism since the revolutions of 1848, Engels himself questioned his earlier analysis:

> History has proved us, and all who thought like us, wrong. It has made it clear that the state of economic development on the Continent at that time was not, by a long way, ripe for the elimination of capitalist production; it has proved this by the economic revolution which, since 1848, has seized the whole of the Continent, and has caused big industry to take real root in France, Austria, Hungary, Poland and recently, in Russia, while it has made Germany positively an industrial country of the first rank—all on a capitalist basis, which in the year 1848, therefore, still had great capacity for expansion. ("Introduction," *Works*, I, 191–92)

Given events of this nature, a theorist of spontaneous revolution is essentially powerless. In virtually all developed European countries, the working class developed consciousness that can be described as social democratic. Social democratic parties, some of which can be traced back to the Second International of 1889, have been in and out of power in virtually all of these. But many of these parties are no longer "socialist" in a strong sense of the term. Rather, their values are largely similar to those of welfare-state liberals in the United States. There is little question that the political success of these parties has improved the lives of workers immensely over the past one hundred fifty years. But the results are still far removed from the deeply moralized end state that Marx envisioned (on which, more shortly). But as a theorist of spontaneous revolution, Marx would have few resources to combat these historical tendencies.

The second criticism is closely related. In a sense analogous to that in which Marx lodged his hopes in spontaneous revolution, he also believed that the revolution would bring about the desired results. Although Marx was reluctant to discuss the details of his future society, he clearly believed that Communism would be qualitatively different from and superior to any society that had existed hitherto. From Marx's occasional remarks we receive glimpses of the future. Classically, in the *German Ideology,* Marx and Engels describe a state in which the division of labor is overcome; under Communism, it is possible "for me to do one thing today and another tomorrow, to hunt in the morning, fish in the afternoon, rear cattle in the evening, [be a critical critic] after dinner, just as I have a mind," without having to practice one of these occupations to the exclusion of others (Tucker, p. 160). Less tantalizing than this Fourierist dream is Marx's account in *Capital,* in which communism means a shortening of the working day, though without rhapsodic airs on changing the nature of labor itself (*Capital,* III, 820). But then again, according to the *Critique of the Gotha Program,* under communism, labor will become "not only a means of life but life's prime want" (*Works,* III, 19). Given the amount and scope of Marx's and Engels's writings, we could present additional quotes and counterquotes, without settling the nature of the future society. But details aside, it is clear that for Marx communism entails a major transformation of human life as it has always been lived. All previous stages of history constitute "the prehistory of human society" (*Works,* I, 504). "Communism is the riddle of history solved and knows itself to be this solution" (Tucker, p. 84). Our riddle is how this transformation is supposed to come about. Even if Marx is right that conflicting forces in capitalist society are going to bring it crashing to the ground and even if he is also right about the revolutionary potential of the proletariat and their ability to take power, it still remains to be explained why proletarian-ruled society will be qualitatively different from all other societies that have existed.

By this point in my inquiries, the depth of this problem should be clear. We have seen that according to Plato, all the resources of the state must be harnessed to the single-minded task of inculcating virtue. People must be educated totally, from the earliest possible moment, throughout their lives. In the *Laws* Plato argues that it is not enough to wait until people are born. If it is to be successful, the process of educating people must begin before they are born. Contrast this with Marx. People are supposed to become good, although the means through which this is supposed to happen are not systematically explored.

In Marx's works there are hints as to how the necessary transformation is to come about.[29] For the most part, Marx's position is that through the process of developing class consciousness, the proletariat will cast aside the disfiguring remnants of the old society. This is in keeping with Marx's view that human nature is essentially plastic. As expressed in the sixth Thesis on Feuerbach: "[T]he human essence is no abstraction inherent in each single individual. In its reality it is the ensemble of the social relations" (*Works,* I, 14). At times, notably in the *German Ideology,* Marx intimates that the process of revolution itself will transform people:

> Both for the production on a mass scale of this communist consciousness, and for the success of the cause itself, the alteration of men on a mass scale is necessary, an alteration which can only take place in a practical movement, a *revolution;* this revolution is necessary, therefore, not only because the *ruling* class cannot be overthrown in any other way, but also because the class *overthrowing* it can only in a revolution succeed in ridding itself of all the muck of ages and become fitted to found society anew. (Tucker, p. 193)

Not only is this claim improbable on its face, but exactly how it is to work is never clearly explained. Couple Marx's faith in spontaneous revolution with his faith that the transformation of human nature will more or less take care of itself, and his theory of radical reform will appear to be inadequate and have as a practical effect leaving the moral status quo intact.

CHAPTER SEVEN

Leninism as Jacobinism

To round out this survey of revolutionary reformers, I examine two currents in the Russian tradition, the revolutionary anarchism of Mikhail Bakunin and then aspects of Lenin's political theory, before and after the Russian Revolution. For our purposes, Bakunin is especially appropriate. In addition to his own distinctive brand of anarchism, he worked out an influential criticism of Marx—to which Marx also wrote a reply. In regard to Lenin, I am especially interested in tracing the stages through which he moved from espousing a modified Marxism to the full-fledged Jacobin position of his final years. Examining the relationship between theory and practice in the thought of this supreme revolutionary practitioner should be a fitting conclusion to this study.

Though considerations of space and scope force me to confine attention to Bakunin and Lenin, we should recognize that doing so does not do full justice to the Russian revolutionary tradition. During the second half of the nineteenth century, much of the Russian intelligentsia entertained hopes for the radical transformation of society. In large part because under tsarist autocracy legal avenues of reform were closed to them, these figures attempted to rouse the masses, whether through propaganda, conspiracies to seize power, or terrorism.[1] Believing in the revolutionary potential and instinctive socialism of the peasants, early Russian populists spurred attempts to "go to the people," to convince the peasants of the wretchedness of their condition and so cause them to rise—"to bring the propaganda of socialism and radical revolution to the masses," to quote Peter Lavrov.[2] But the people were not receptive to this message, often turning over their would-be liberators to the Tsar's police.

In response to the failure of peaceful tactics, radicals turned to Jacobin-like conspiracy theories associated with Peter Tkachev, which are widely believed to have had a strong influence on Lenin.[3] The terrorist wing of Russian radicalism had considerable success at assassinating public officials, most notably Tsar Alexander II, in 1881, murdered by *Narodnaya Volya,* the People's Will. According to Sophia Perovskaya, one of the assassins: "The peasantry, oppressed by hard life, suffering from hunger, and *expecting an improvement in its situation only from the tsar,* upon hearing that the old one had been killed and the new one had been too or was about to be, and that all power has passed into the hands of the 'lords,' would rise."[4] But such alchemy of Revolution was not able to turn lead into gold.

We begin with Bakunin, who in his underlying assumptions represents Russian populism at its most radical—and most unrealistic.

Bakunin

Although Marx supported generally spontaneous revolution, with little role for an enlightened elite, his view was criticized for Jacobin tendencies by Bakunin, who was his contemporary and political rival in the Socialist International. Bakunin is more important as a political actor than a political thinker. He took part in numerous revolutionary movements during the mid-nineteenth century, paying for his activity with extended confinement in the Peter and Paul Fortress, before being exiled to Siberia and escaping eastward to the United States and then Europe to resume his career. Throughout his life Bakunin was constantly joining and forming organizations committed to toppling existing power structures. In both academic and popular imaginations, he epitomizes the anarchist as revolutionary activist, as expressed in his most famous pronouncement: "The urge to destroy is a creative urge."[5] A timeless descrip-

tion of Bakunin in action is provided by the great Russian émigré writer
Alexander Herzen:

> [Bakunin] argued, preached, gave orders, shouted, decided, arranged,
> organized, exhorted, the whole day, the whole night, the whole twenty-
> four hours on end. In the brief moments which remained, he would
> throw himself down on his desk, sweep a small space clear of to-
> bacco ash, and begin to write ten, fifteen letters. . . . In the middle
> of a letter he would throw down his pen in order to refute some re-
> actionary Dalmation; then, without finishing his speech, he would
> seize his pen and go on writing. . . . His activity, his appetite, like all
> other characteristics—even his gigantic size and continual sweat—
> were of superhuman proportions.[6]

As a theorist, Bakunin was largely derivative, combining disparate
themes from other thinkers, mainly Hegel and Marx, and rarely complet-
ing the ambitious theoretical projects he set for himself. He was not a systematic thinker, and so the attempt here to lay out some of his central
themes in straightforward fashion is somewhat misleading, an imposition of order on relative chaos. But in spite of his works' shortcomings,
Bakunin developed significant insights. In addition to his dispute with
Marx, he addressed central paradoxes in the theory of spontaneous revolution and the role of revolutionary organizations in popular rebellion.

Central to Bakunin's thought is desire for freedom. He views the two
main opponents of freedom as God and the state—to give the title of
one of his most famous works. Following Ludwig Feuerbach, he views
God as a fictitious entity, created by human beings and used by particular people to oppress others. Rephrasing Voltaire's famous remark,
Bakunin declares that "if God really existed, it would be necessary to
abolish him" (*GS,* p. 28).[7]

Like God, the state too is born of oppression and necessarily entails oppression: "If there is a state there is necessarily domination and
consequently slavery. A state without slavery, open or camouflaged, is
inconceivable—that is why we are enemies of the state" (*SA,* p. 178). The
state is insidious in providing the opportunity for domination. Because it
is inherent in mankind to take advantage of opportunities offered, the

only way to end domination is to abolish the political forms that allow it to exist. To a large extent Bakunin was an anarchist because of his low opinion of human nature. It is because political power necessarily corrupts that it must be abolished.

The central question of Bakunin's political theory is how to accomplish this. Like other thinkers discussed in this work, Bakunin is deeply concerned with the means required to move from present society to a preferred future condition. But he insists that the means not be political in the conventional sense. Although he recognizes that the existing power structure will not topple by itself and so must be forcibly overthrown, this must be accomplished without creating new political institutions that are subject to the same abuse as the old. Thus the only form acceptable to Bakunin is spontaneous popular rebellion. To the extent that the people rise without the benefit of organized guidance, they need not fear betrayal by their leaders. When the revolution has succeeded and political bodies have been destroyed, the victorious revolutionaries must lay down their arms and begin to organize society anew.

Bakunin is a committed socialist. The freedom he desires requires elimination of economic inequalities and so overthrow of existing economic as well as political structures. Because this too must be accomplished without bringing into existence institutions that are subject to abuse, once again, the revolution must be spontaneous and not create new centers of power.

Bakunin develops his position in opposition to two alternative paths, which he identifies as forms of "state socialism." In each case the movement to the new society is to be in two stages. In the first stage, the socialists seize control of the state; in the second, they use state power to overturn existing economic arrangements. The two forms of state socialism differ in how they aim to seize the state. Democratic socialism, which Bakunin identifies with Ferdinand Lassalle, argues that the state can be taken over by the working class through democratic processes. Revolutionary socialists, a category in which Bakunin includes Marx, propose forcible seizure of political power. Bakunin differs from adherents of both these positions in opposing the idea of first taking power and then using it. A new group must not be allowed to grasp the state in either of these ways. The revolution must not *seize* the state but must *smash* it. The same process, moreover, that destroys the state must destroy the economy as well. Bakunin describes his program in an 1870 letter written to Sergei Nechaev:

> The programme can be clearly expressed in a few words: total destruction of the framework of state and law and of the whole of the so-called bourgeois civilization by a spontaneous people's revolution. (*OV,* p. 6).

Bakunin objects to the two-stage models because of their liability to abuse. Would-be revolutionaries, whether democratic socialists or revolutionary socialists, will not move on to the second stage. Once they control political power, they will use it for their own ends, thereby perpetuating the abuse of power that is integral to all states.

We can set aside the details of Bakunin's criticisms of democratic socialism. His objection to Marx's position — or what he views as this — centers on the dictatorship of the proletariat. In keeping with his overall fear of state power, Bakunin believes that the Marxian revolution will not smash the state but will give rise to a new form of state, the dictatorship of the proletariat. As I have noted, Marx views this as only a transitional form, destined to wither away. But Bakunin views the dictatorship of the proletariat as political rule and so necessarily corrupting and oppressive. Even though the ruling group will be comprised of workers, they will engage in the same oppression encountered throughout history:

> [F]rom whatever point of view we look at this question, it always comes down to the same dismal result: government of the vast majority of the people by a privileged minority. But this minority, the Marxists say, will consist of workers. Yet, perhaps of *former* workers, who, as soon as they become rulers or representatives of the people will cease to be workers and will begin to look upon the whole workers' world from the heights of the state. (*SA,* p. 178)

Why does Bakunin think this will happen? "Anyone who doubts this is not familiar with human nature" (*SA,* p. 178).

From the Marxian standpoint, parts of Bakunin's argument are nonsensical. If the dictatorship of the proletariat is a form of rule, Bakunin argues, it must be rule *over* someone else. Bakunin proposes that this will be the proletariat over the peasants, or, from a national point of view, Germans over Slavs (*SA*, pp. 177–78). Marx's response to these claims: "Schoolboy drivel!"[8] We have seen that Marx never viewed proletarian dictatorship as rule by a vanguard party. Thus Bakunin's criticism of Marx for being a Jacobin is off base.

Still even if Marx was not a Jacobin, Bakunin presents a trenchant critique of Jacobinism as a path to a better society. Because power will always be abused, the successful revolution must not create structures of authority. The people must liberate themselves: "Liberty can be created only by liberty" (*SA*, p. 179). "We believe that the people can be happy and free only when they create their own life, organizing themselves from below upward by means of independent and completely free associations, subject to no official tutelage but open to the free and diverse influences of individuals and parties" (*SA*, p. 136).

Bakunin is especially suspicious of certain kinds of revolutionaries, whom he characterizes as political metaphysicians. Such figures attempt to impose their ideas on the people instead of being led by the people's wishes. Government by a group who claim to *know* what is in everyone else's best interests is a recipe for catastrophe. Let a scholar govern, "and he will become the most unbearable tyrant, for scholarly pride is repulsive, offensive, and more oppressive than any other. To be the slaves of pedants—what a fate for mankind" (*SA*, p. 134). As Paul Thomas observes, Bakunin viewed theory itself as an oppressive force, ranged along with religion and political authority on the opposite side of a great divide from life, spontaneity, and creative urges.[9] Intellectuals in power, as new Procrustes, will twist their fellow men to shape, "whatever the cost" (*SA*, p. 133). One of Bakunin's central principles is that people's consciousness must form the basis for revolution rather than be created by revolutionaries.

The dangers Bakunin fears can be avoided if the revolution is spontaneous, flowing from the people's revolutionary consciousness. Having swept away existing political forms and overturned society, the people will be able to create a new society, founded on free, spontaneous organization. Like Marx, then, Bakunin is able to avoid a series of theoretical difficulties by positing spontaneous revolution. But as is the case with Marx, his position is defensible only if the longed-for revolution will actually come about.

Like other proponents of spontaneous revolution, Bakunin faces the problem of prompting the people to rebel. He is optimistic on this score. Like other Russian populists, he believes that the people are instinctively revolutionary. Long experience of oppression has convinced them of the need to rebel and that they must liberate themselves. They realize that leaving state power intact will result in more oppression in the future and so that the state must be smashed. Bakunin also believes that popular consciousness solves the problem of organizing socialism in the future society. He falls in the tradition of Russian populism in believing that the traditional Russian peasant commune, the *mir,* will be the basis for future communities. Because the people are instinctively committed to this, they will develop socialist forms of their own accord, after the revolution.

Because of his reluctance to impose revolutionary ideas on the people, Bakunin believes that the revolution must wait on popular consciousness. But in this respect too he is optimistic. He believes that the people are ready to rebel and so foresees only a limited role for an organization of revolutionaries:

> [W]e have neither the intention nor the least desire to impose on our own people or on any other an ideal social organization that we have drawn from books or thought up on our own. In the belief that the masses bear all the elements of their future organizational norms in their own more or less historically evolved instincts, in their everyday needs and their conscious and unconscious desires, we seek that ideal within the people themselves. (*SA,* p. 135)

But still there is need for organization. Though the people are instinctively revolutionary and on the point of rising, they cannot bring off a successful revolution of their own accord. We should note that if they could do this all theoretical problems would be solved. One need only sit back and watch as the people reach the boiling point, rise up, and, after dispatching their opponents, create the new society. But all this cannot happen unless a revolutionary organization coordinates the people's efforts, directing them, like an army's general staff. But given what we have seen, Bakunin is afraid that if the organization has authority to direct the people, its members will become oppressors. Even if the revolution succeeds, it will merely result in a new body of officials lording it over the people.

Thus Bakunin believes that the committed revolutionary must tread a narrow path. On the one hand, he must avoid passivity. Not taking action and waiting for the revolution to break out will result in its non-occurrence. On the other hand, an authoritative structure capable of directing the people toward their revolutionary goal will invariably lead to the goal's being subverted. Thus there is need for organization, but not too much, and organization of a distinctive kind. As the organization's aim "is not the creation of new States or new despotisms but rather the radical destruction of all private dominions, its character and its organization must be essentially different from those of the States."[10]

Bakunin has two main ideas for the requisite new kind of organization. Although authority is needed, only a special kind is acceptable. Rather than a structure based on formal relationships of hierarchy and subordination, the revolutionary organization must depend on *natural* authority. Unlike traditional authority, natural authority is freely accepted. By virtue of their superior moral characteristics, the members of the revolutionary organization must be looked up to by the people, who follow them voluntarily:

> In general, we ask nothing better than to see men endowed with great knowledge, great experience, great minds, and, above all, great hearts, exercise over us a natural and legitimate influence, freely accepted, and never imposed in the name of any official authority whatsoever, celestial or terrestrial. We accept all natural authorities and all influences of fact, but none of right; for every authority or every influence of right, officially imposed as such, becoming directly an oppression and a falsehood, would inevitably impose upon us, as I believe I have sufficiently shown, slavery and absurdity. (*GS*, p. 35)

Key to acceptance of natural authority is the overwhelming virtue of the revolutionaries. Bakunin describes this in impossibly idealistic terms—

although, we should note, he was virtually indiscriminate in regard to his actual revolutionary associates (as his dealings with Sergei Nechaev show). The organization must be made up of

> persons who are most determined, *most intelligent and as far as possible knowledgeable, i.e., intelligent by experience,* who are passionately and undeviatingly devoted, who have, as far as possible, renounced all personal interests and have renounced once and for all, for life, or for death itself, all that attracts people, all material comforts and delights, all satisfaction of ambition, status, and fame. They must be totally and wholly absorbed by one passion, the people's liberation. They must be persons who would renounce personal historical importance while they are alive and even a name in history after their death. (*OV,* p. 28)

This "complete self-denial" can exist only in the presence of passion. "Passion alone can bring about this miracle within a man, this strength without effort" (*OV,* p. 28).

We could go on, but the point should be clear. Not having substantial grounds on which to base his nonauthoritative organization, Bakunin falls back on prodigies of human nature. Because people have an inherent tendency to abuse their power, he must rely on a genus of people who will not do so. But aside from this group's extraordinary virtue, Bakunin has no solution to his problem. His eventual position recalls the great soul of Rousseau's lawgiver—who overcomes all obstacles to the new society through force of personality.

Alongside Bakunin's idea of authority that is not authority is his second main idea, to which we can refer as the "disorganized conspiracy." We have seen that the revolution must be organized in various ways. Even if the people rise up spontaneously, activities in different geographic areas must be coordinated. Again, the analogy is an army's general staff. Bakunin describes this as a "collective dictatorship": "An invisible force—recognized by no one—through which the collective dictatorship of our organization will be the mightier, the more it remains invisible and unacknowledged, the more it remains without any official legality and significance" (*OV,* p. 26). The invisible dictatorship, based on natural as opposed to official authority, is necessary to organize the spontaneously erupting movements in different places. As the Russian people rise and destroy the state and the entire sociopolitical order, the "enormous quantity of mud which has accumulated within the people is stirred and rises to the surface. . . . It seems this is a terrible and hopeless anarchy" (*OV*, pp. 26–27). Anarchy must be channeled in constructive directions, and this is the role of the collective dictatorship.

But once again, Bakunin confronts the possibility that power will be abused. We have seen that permissible authority must be only natural and so freely accepted. But is this enough? As a further guarantee against abuse of authority, Bakunin argues for lack of organization in the collective dictatorship. Instead of being organized through a chain of command, its activity will be directed by a plan:

> The dictatorship is not contrary to the free development and self-determination of the people, or its organization from below according to its own customs and instincts for it acts on the people only by the natural personal influence of its members who are not invested with any power and are scattered like an invisible net in all regions, districts, and rural communities and, each one in his own place and in agreement with others, trying to direct the spontaneous revolutionary movement of the people towards a general plan which has been fully agreed and defined beforehand. (*OV*, 27–28)

In keeping with his insistence that the revolution be based on the people's own ideas, that the revolutionary organization not foist its consciousness on them, Bakunin views the plan in question as a codification of popular consciousness. In this sense, his view of the relationship between spontaneous revolution and organizing forces is similar to Marx's. The organization is charged with developing and extending the people's consciousness instead of concocting a theory of its own. But fearing too active a role by the organization, Bakunin argues that much of this coordinating function must be performed by the plan rather than through direct human agency. Thus the revolution's true general staff is the plan that directs the organization. So conceived, the plan has to be an extraordinary concoction:

The plan for the organization of the people's liberty must firstly be firmly and clearly delineated as regards its main principles and aims in order to exclude any possibility of misunderstanding and deviation by its members who will be called upon to help in its realization. Secondly, it must be sufficiently wide and human to embrace and take in all the inescapable changes which arise from differing circumstances, all varied movements arising from the variety of national life. (*OV*, p. 28)

[The secret organization is] firmly united: inspired by a common ideal and a common aim which are applied everywhere, of course modified according to prevailing conditions: an organization which acts everywhere according to a common plan. (*OV*, p. 27)

Bakunin's reasoning is clearly far-fetched. The requisite degrees of specificity and flexibility are not compatible. It is possible to imagine a plan sufficiently rigid to direct revolutionaries throughout all of Russia. But such rigidity is obviously incompatible with the kind of tactical flexibility one needs to act effectively in a fluid political situation. Then again, one can imagine a plan that is sufficiently flexible to allow tactical adjustments. But this will lack the clear focus needed to coordinate activities over a large area. Under ordinary circumstances, an actual general staff might be able to combine the two imperatives. It could have clear objectives in mind, which it attempts to realize by adjusting strategy to changing circumstances. As we ordinarily imagine such things, a military force will be able to adjust rapidly to changing circumstances only if there is a strict chain of command and orders are quickly carried out. But of course Bakunin fears a general staff that has such authority and discretion. His own attempt to square the circle is to recognize the need for organization and to posit the requisite organizing force but then to require that this be structured in such a way that it could not function. Forced to sail between the Scylla of lack of organization and the Charybdis of an effective organization but with the potential of abuse, Bakunin posits unorganized organization, or again, what we can term the disorganized conspiracy. Even if we grant all his assumptions about the people's consciousness and revolutionary potential, the revolution cannot succeed, because the necessary organization comprises self-contradictory elements.

Bakunin is not alone in facing the need to work between Scylla and Charybdis. This has long been the bane of supporters of popular revolution. Spontaneous revolution has the great virtue of allowing the people to liberate themselves, without fear that their efforts will be subverted by their leaders. But if the people are actually so revolutionary, there is little point in theorizing about it; one must ask, if this is actually a possibility, why have they not yet revolted? As noted at the beginning of this chapter, different Russian populists proposed different means to awaken the people, ranging from propaganda to terrorist acts — propaganda by deed. But Bakunin raises the question: when the people have risen, why has this not resulted in true freedom? The obvious response is that the underlying problem is misestimation of the people's potential. Although there have been risings that could be termed spontaneous — in Russia alone in 1905, 1917, and perhaps 1989, and perhaps also the abortive uprisings of Stenka Razin and Pugachev[11] — these had relatively specific political goals, especially to topple oppressive governments. But with the old system brought down, the people hardly seem situated to agree on and act on a new one that is qualitatively different from what has gone before. The uncharitable response to Bakunin is that the urge to destroy is just that, an urge to destroy the existing order, without clear implications in regard to what to put in its place.

Bakunin's claim that the people are instinctively revolutionary and instinctively socialist is wishful thinking — much as we saw in regard to Marx. But if the people are not spontaneously revolutionary, what is to be done? The true revolutionary must combat the people's complacency. But as Bakunin timelessly asks, if the people must be pushed, who will protect them from the pushers? As we see in the next section, Lenin's career is bound up with different struggles against the people's lack of revolutionary potential, eventuating in a distinctly Jacobin position.

Leninism as Jacobinism

The evolution of Lenin's political thought represents a case study in the problems of spontaneous revolution and the attraction of Jacobin ideas.

Early in his career, Lenin began to assume the series of positions I have identified as Jacobinism:

(J.1) A plan or blueprint of the desired, ideal society;

(J.2) A low estimation of the vast majority of the inhabitants of existing society in regard to their ability to realize (J.1);

(J.3) Belief in the existence of a small group of individuals who understand the blueprint and are strongly committed to its realization;

(J.4) Support of this group's, this minority's, seizure of political power;

(J.5) Use of the minority-controlled state to condition and reeducate the inhabitants of society;

(J.6) A distinctive theory of representation, which we can call "real representation."

It is not surprising that other Russian social democrats, notably Trotsky, criticized Lenin for Jacobinism, as they understood this. Trotsky complained that Lenin's "'absolute belief in a metaphysical idea' was accompanied by an 'absolute disbelief in living people.'"[12] This accusation was first lodged against Lenin in connection with his views on party organization, as given classic expression in *What Is to Be Done?* In this work, Lenin presents a pessimistic assessment of the revolutionary potential of the working class. Left to themselves, the workers will become reformists rather than revolutionaries: "The history of all countries shows that the working class, exclusively by its own effort, is able to develop only trade union consciousness" (*SW*, I, 143).[13] Accordingly, Lenin argues for the importance of leadership, of a tightly disciplined party, to see that the workers are properly led and imbued with the most advanced revolutionary theory. In contrast to other thinkers who extol the revolutionary potential of the masses, Lenin takes the radical step of arguing that the party must *combat* spontaneity: "our task, the task of Social Democracy, is to *combat spontaneity,* to *divert* the working-class movement" from their spontaneous tendency toward trade-union consciousness, to care for their own economic advancement, rather than for revolution (*SW*, I, 151).

Lenin's position here carries him beyond Marx's view of the relationship between theory and practice. One of Lenin's governing assumptions is that a correct revolutionary theory has been developed and should be applied to conditions in Russia. Among other qualifications for party membership is understanding of and adherence to this theory, which is emphatically declared to be above criticism. Though this is not stated explicitly, the unmistakable implication of Lenin's position is that the unity of theory and practice has been severed. Theory exists prior to and independent of practice, as a guide to practice.[14] The extent to which practice is able reciprocally to influence theory is not clear.

Thus in *What Is to Be Done?* Lenin approaches a Jacobin synthesis. He commits himself to some version of (J.1), the ideal plan, (J.2), a low opinion of the people's potential, and (J.3), the minority that is able to grasp true theory. But the other elements are not present. Lenin does not discuss (J.4), the need for the minority to seize political power, and so (J.5) and (J.6), the minority-controlled state educating the people and representing their real interests, are not discussed either. It seems that Lenin stops short of Jacobinism in this work because his disillusionment with the people is not complete. Though he believes that they require guidance in order to attain political awareness, the necessary tutelage can occur within existing society. Under the guidance of a properly organized party with correct revolutionary theory, the working class will be able to achieve the necessary consciousness and make the revolution themselves. And so at this point in Lenin's career, the revolution is to be accomplished by the workers as well as for them. Presumably, when victory has been won, they will be able to take charge of their own political affairs. This reading of Lenin's views in *What Is to Be Done?* and the following years is supported by detailed analysis of his subsequent writings in which he expresses greater faith in the masses' spontaneous development, the conviction that they will eventually grasp socialist ideas themselves.[15]

Something along these basic lines remains Lenin's position until the October Revolution. This is seen in the analysis of revolutionary politics in *State and Revolution,* which of course was written only months before Lenin's ascent to power. For our purposes, what is most striking about this tract is Lenin's analysis of the dictatorship of the proletariat.

Lenin places considerable emphasis on the dictatorship of the proletariat in this work, calling it the "touchstone" on which true understanding of Marxism should be tested, "undoubtedly" the most important part of Marx's and Engels's theory (*SW,* II, 311, 302). The argument in *State and Revolution* is mainly commentary on Marx's and Engels's discussions of the nature of the state and revolutionary politics, and Lenin's characterization of the dictatorship in this work is generally faithful to Marx and Engels. Lenin too argues that the institutions that make up the dictatorship of the proletariat are to be in the hands of the working class as a whole. All previous states boiled down to the minority ruling over the vast majority; here for the first time the majority will be in power. The particular institutions of the dictatorship, modeled on the Paris Commune as described in Marx's *Civil War in France,* are designed to place the workers in direct control of state affairs. Lenin goes so far as to advocate the elimination of police and administrative functionaries to accomplish this (esp. *State and Revolution,* chap. 3).

Lenin's understanding of the major functions of the dictatorship is also similar to Marx's. It has two main tasks: first, to protect the revolution from its enemies; second, to organize and develop the postrevolutionary economy.[16] For ease of reference, in the remainder of this chapter I refer to the first of these tasks as "negative" and to the second as "positive." In *State and Revolution* Lenin's emphasis falls more heavily on the negative side. For instance, he says at one point that the "working people need the state *only* to suppress the resistance of the exploiters" (II, 303).

A few important, unresolved ambiguities are found in this tract. First, although *State and Revolution* is unusual among Lenin's works in paying little attention to the Party, this is not entirely absent, though the extent of its role in the revolution is not specified. Lenin is unclear as to whether the vanguard of the proletariat or the proletariat as a whole is to play the leading role in the revolution. At one point he describes the proletariat as the *leader* of the exploited and oppressed people rather than as a major constituent of these groups (II, 304). But in the one context in which Lenin mentions the vanguard of the proletariat, that is, the Party, he assigns it the task of leading the whole people to socialism (II, 304). Another ambiguity in Lenin's position is suggested by his assigning the dictatorship of the proletariat—and perhaps the vanguard as the leading element in this—additional, vague positive functions. It is to be "the teacher, the guide, the leader of all the working and exploited people in organizing their social life without the bourgeoisie and against the bourgeoisie" (II, 304).

Thus we see that Lenin's view in *State and Revolution* is not entirely without ambiguities. The elements discussed in the last paragraph conflict with the anarchistic orientation of the tract as a whole, but too much should not be made of them. It seems that until the October Revolution at least, Lenin was not a Jacobin. His considered position was that political power should be used after the revolution mainly to crush the resistance of the bourgeoisie. He had not yet embraced the Jacobin conviction that the masses could not rule themselves until they had undergone a rigorous process of state-controlled education and conditioning by the enlightened minority—although I will qualify this claim in regard to the Russian peasantry shortly.

Within a few months, when Lenin confronted the grave situation in Russia after the October Revolution, he began to move away from his earlier positions. It seems that in the immediate aftermath of the revolution Lenin made at least some effort to put into practice his understanding of Marxian political theory. In his influential study of Lenin's political theory, Neil Harding makes a convincing case that during this period at least, Lenin was motivated by the radical ideas of *State and Revolution*.[17] As Harding argues, in the months following the seizure of power, "Lenin set himself the task of encouraging a revolution more radical than any the world has seen before or since. The stated object of that revolution was emphatically not the capture and consolidation of state power but rather the dissolution of the state itself."[18] At the Party's Seventh Congress, in March 1918, Lenin argued for moving beyond existing state institutions, to allow the people to participate in government and, in doing so, to gain proper consciousness:

> All citizens must take part in the work of the courts and in the government of the country. It is important for us to draw literally all working people into the government of the state. It is a task of tremendous difficulty. But socialism cannot be implemented by a minority, by the Party. It can be implemented only by tens of millions when they have learned to do it themselves. (*SW*, II, 612–13)

Workers also took active part in controlling industrial production. And so Lenin apparently tried to realize the anarchistic ideals of *State and*

Revolution. Thus in November and December 1917, Lenin declared that
the postrevolutionary government would be in the hands of the working
classes as a whole, and during this period he believed that revolutionary
activity would be transformative.[19] The government would exist mainly to
crush the proletariat's class enemies.

But Lenin quickly became aware of the impossibility of such administrative measures under the conditions existing in Russia. In the economic sphere, he turned increasingly to factory managers. In government
he began to build formidable coercive mechanisms, especially a reconsti-
tuted military and the Cheka, the secret police. In practice and then in
theory, Lenin began to substitute the rule of the Party for the rule of the
working class. Opposing political parties were excluded from power, and
though Lenin was reluctant to admit that the Party exercised real power,
all opposing forces were soon crushed.[20]

In the period following the October Revolution, Lenin's understanding of the dictatorship of the proletariat underwent a clear process of
development. A series of positive functions were added to its original
negative role, until it eventually evolved into something recognizable as
the Jacobin, positive, educative state. It falls beyond the scope of this
study to analyze specific developments during this tumultuous period in
Russia, and specific steps in the evolution of Lenin's ideas are not easy to
make out—in part because, as a political leader, he often did not wish to
advertise them. In large part Lenin was responding to changing political
conditions, especially the recalcitrance of the Russian peasantry, who
constituted the overwhelming majority of the population and were not
socialist either consciously or instinctively. Clearly, by implication at least,
in deciding to seize power in an overwhelmingly peasant, underdevel-
oped country, Lenin had committed himself to some version of Jacobin
politics from the outset of the revolution. An extended historical period
and extensive state control would be necessary to develop the revolutionary consciousness of the peasantry.[21] Although Lenin was responsible for
important theoretical developments in regard to incorporating a significant role for the peasantry into Marxian revolutionary theory,[22] it is difficult to say how clearly he consciously confronted the implications of the
peasants' condition during the period before the seizure of power. But
once the Bolsheviks controlled the state, the problems of the peasantry

were brought front and center. Dealing with the peasants' resistance to Communism became of paramount concern. In the words of Adam Ulam: "Somewhere between 1917 and 1921 the Communist struggle ceased to be merely a struggle against the Whites and foreign intervention and became also a fight against the way of life, habits, and ideas of a vast majority of the Russian people and not merely those of the *bourgeoisie* and the *kulaks* [i.e., the so-called rich peasants]."[23] The revolution had been made in good part on the promise of land to the peasants, to quote Ulam once again, "by promising the peasant something [the Russian Marxists] did not believe in, the untouchability of his property."[24]

Roughly and briefly, Lenin's analysis of the peasantry was based on distinctions among different classes: poor, middle, and rich peasants. The conjunction of interests between the poor peasants and the proletariat had been a centerpiece of his thought since his earliest writings,[25] and it was because of the fundamental opposition of interests between the poor and rich peasants that, in October 1919, Lenin described the demarcation of peasant classes as "the whole *essence* of socialism" (*SW*, III, 294). But by this time Lenin recognized the backward condition of the entire peasant class. Because they were property owners as well as workers, the peasants' allegiance vacillated between the proletariat and bourgeoisie. Thus it was essential that the proletariat lead them (*SW*, III, 296).[26] Lenin's gradual loss of faith in the revolutionary potential of the poor peasants, along with that of the proletariat as well, led him to embrace full-fledged Jacobinism.

Keeping the details of the political situation in the background, we can distinguish three rough stages in the development of Lenin's view of the dictatorship of the proletariat. Though the stages were not entirely distinct chronologically, for our purposes, it is necessary to sort them out. First, in the immediate aftermath of the October Revolution, Lenin argued that the dictatorship of the proletariat had essentially negative functions. For instance, in *The Proletarian Revolution and the Renegade Kautsky*, written approximately one year after the October Revolution, he states: "The revolutionary dictatorship of the proletariat is rule, won and maintained by the use of violence by the proletariat against the bourgeoisie rule that is unrestricted by any laws" (*SW*, III, 75).

Why do we need a dictatorship when we have a majority? And Marx and Engels explain:

—to break down the resistance of the bourgeoisie;

—to inspire the reactionaries with fear;

—to maintain the authority of the armed people against the bourgeoisie;

—that the proletariat may forcibly hold down its adversaries. (III, 88)

Second, Lenin eventually came to hold the position that the proletarian state must perform dual tasks. It had coercive functions but was also responsible for constructing a socialist society. By early 1919 the second position was explicitly advanced. In the third stage, Lenin emphasized the positive functions at the expense of the negative, justifying rule by the proletariat (or by the Party) as necessary primarily because of its constructive and educative tasks.

Though hints can be detected earlier, Lenin first explicitly addressed the "low cultural level" of the Russian workers as a factor impeding the development of socialism in January 1918.[27] A clear example of the dual tasks of the dictatorship of the proletariat is found in Lenin's "Greetings to the Hungarian Workers," written in May 1919. Having described the dictatorship's negative role, crushing the formerly exploiting classes, Lenin places more weight on the positive side:

But the essence of proletarian dictatorship is not in force alone, or even mainly in force. Its chief feature is the organization and discipline of the advanced contingent of the working people, of their vanguard; of their sole leader, the proletariat, whose object is to build socialism, abolish the division of society into classes, make all members of society working people, and remove the basis for all exploitation of man by man. (*SW*, III, 216)

The dictatorship of the proletariat must take the lead in performing these tasks, because the general run of people cannot be trusted to guide themselves. They are powerfully bound by the force of habit, by "the habit of running things in a petty bourgeois and bourgeois way," "shackled very much by petty bourgeois habits and traditions." This causes them to resist the transition to socialism (III, 216). The idea that the force of habit is an obstacle to socialism, and so must be combated, is a major theme in Lenin's political thought from this point on.

The two-sided function of the dictatorship of the proletariat is also discussed in "A Great Beginning," written in June 1919. Here too the positive function takes precedence over the negative:

> It was natural and inevitable in the first period after the proletarian revolution that we should be engaged primarily on the main and fundamental task of overcoming the resistance of the bourgeoisie, of vanquishing the exploiters, of crushing their conspiracy. . . . But simultaneously with this task, another task comes to the forefront just as inevitably and ever more imperatively as time goes on, namely the more important task of positive communist construction, the creation of new economic relations, of a new society. (*SW*, III, 229)[28]

Here too the major bar to the construction of socialism is the mind-set of the masses. In order for an industrial economy to be built, the working people must voluntarily submit to the necessary discipline. Because they resist, a massive reshaping of minds is called for:

> [I]t is necessary to overcome the resistance (frequently passive, which is particularly stubborn and particularly difficult to overcome) of the numerous survivals of small scale production; it is necessary to overcome the enormous force of habit and conservatism which are connected with these survivals. (*SW*, III, 231)[29]

The need to overcome the force of habit bears fruit in a series of linked ideas that are essentially Jacobin. First, as we have seen, the force of habit must be combated and the mass of the people reeducated and remolded. Second, this process of remolding will take a very long time. Third, the task of fighting the force of habit must be left to the Party. Fourth, to accomplish this, all the resources of the state are needed, and so it is necessary not to weaken the dictatorship of the proletariat. All of these themes coalesce in *"Left Wing" Communism—An Infantile Disorder,* written in April 1920. I quote a single paragraph, which indicates how strongly Jacobinism had taken hold:

> The dictatorship of the proletariat means a persistent struggle—bloody and bloodless, violent and peaceful, military and economic, educational and administrative—against the forces and traditions of the old society. The force of habit in millions and tens of millions is a most formidable force. Without a party of iron that has been tempered in the struggle, a party enjoying the confidence of all honest people in the class in question, a party capable of watching and influencing the mood of the masses, such a struggle cannot be waged successfully. (*SW,* III, 368)

Lenin's concern with the force of habit leads to the remarkable assertion (for a Marxist) that this alone is capable of restoring bourgeois society and bourgeois rule. Though the big bourgeoisie have been vanquished and both the means of production and state power are firmly in the hands of the proletariat, unless the force of habit is dealt with, it produces "the *very* result which the bourgeoisie need and which tends to *restore* the bourgeoisie." Any weakening of the dictatorship of the proletariat, then, actually aids the bourgeoisie against the proletariat.[30]

In *"Left Wing" Communism,* Lenin lets slip the facade of rule by the proletariat as a class. The emphasis is on Party control. Though Lenin is on the whole reluctant to admit that the proletarian state is government for rather than *by* the working class,[31] he reveals this in other works as well. For instance, at the Eighth Party Congress, in March 1919, he states that the section of the workers who are actually governing is "inordinately, incredibly small" (*SW,* III, 182).[32] Rule by the Party is justified by a combination of the backwardness of the masses and the superior moral and intellectual qualities of the Party members.[33]

In light of the educative tasks assigned to the dictatorship of the proletariat, it is not surprising that Lenin pays increased attention to the mechanics of education and culture. In two striking pieces written in October 1920, he takes these themes to their logical conclusion. In "On Proletarian Culture," he declares that since Marxism has proved to be the only true expression of the interests and culture of the proletariat, the Party and other proletarian organizations (controlled by the Party) should assume a leading role in all public education (*SW,* III, 484–85). In "The Tasks of the Youth Leagues," Lenin discusses these matters in detail. Great claims are made for the intellectual preeminence of Marxism, which represents an assimilation of and development on the sum of human knowledge. Accordingly, it is of the utmost importance that the youth of the new society be brought to understand Marxism. Lenin introduces an important distinction here, between generations. The task of the old generation, brought up under capitalism, was to destroy the existing society. Brought up in a society dominated by bourgeois intellectual processes, this generation is unable completely to move beyond them. The work of building a new society falls to a new generation. This task demands new education:

> Only by radically remolding the teaching, organization and training of the youth shall we be able to ensure that the efforts of the younger generation will result in the creation of a society that will be unlike the old society, i.e., in the creation of communist society. (*SW,* III, 470–71; see pp. 470–83)

Thus the dictatorship of the proletariat must last for at least a generation until the youth can be properly educated and brought to the promised land.

Educational philosophy in the early years of the Soviet regime reflected this need. Anatoli Lunacharsky headed the People's Commisariat for Education after the October Revolution. In the speech "The Philosophy of the School and the Revolution," delivered in May 1923, he declared that the goal of education is "the one miracle that science can recognize—the transformation of the human race."[34] "Re-education is necessary, sometimes through a severe purging of oneself and of others around one. We have to be freed from all the 'opium' that was once poured into our veins, from all the egoism and dead weight of prejudices that handicap each one of us" (p. 165). These themes are basic to Lunacharsky's position, stated repeatedly in his speeches both before and after Lenin died. For instance, in "Education of the New Man," delivered in May 1928: "for us true education means just that, the education of a new kind of human being, since the old variety, educated in a chaotic and uncultured capitalist society, is unsatisfactory" (p. 222). In "Educational Tasks of the Soviet School," delivered in June 1928: "The re-education of adults and education of young people and children are the precondition for further economic and political successes, not to mention that it is they that bring about the transformation of human life which gives true meaning to the whole movement of the proletariat" (p. 243). Needless to say, this massive educative task falls to the Party and organizations under Party control.

CONSEQUENCES

At this point it should be clear how far Lenin's position evolved from that of Marx. There is little doubt that by 1920—if not earlier—Lenin had become a full-fledged Jacobin. He subscribed to all six of the points that constitute Jacobinism. He believed that Marxism held the key to a perfect society (and so J.1) but that the vast majority of people were incapable of grasping this (and so J.2). As we have seen, between his early and late works, Lenin came to realize that the masses could not be given proper consciousness in existing society and so must be educated by all the resources of the state. What is particularly striking in this regard is his conviction that individuals brought up in a corrupt society are incorrigible. True consciousness is beyond their grasp, and so the work of building socialism falls to the next generation. Lenin of course believed in the Party, the organization of committed revolutionaries, imbued with correct theory (and so J.3). Similarly, he supported the Party's seizure of power (and so J.4), though he was reluctant to admit that Party rule was not rule by the proletariat as a whole. Finally, he believed in the need for the postrevolutionary state to educate the bulk of the population (and so J.5), while he also approached an explicit statement of the view that the Party was justified in holding power because it represented the interests of society as a whole (i.e., J.6).

These points seem to be well established, and their implications are clear. Because Marx believed that the working class must liberate itself, his theory bars a certain outcome. It goes against Marx's entire outlook to legitimize a postrevolutionary dictatorship of the few empowered to educate the many. Accordingly, Lenin's loss of faith in the ability of the masses to achieve revolutionary consciousness is of the last consequence, bearing fruit in exactly the kind of postrevolutionary state that Bakunin feared.

The implications of Lenin's modifications of Marx's political theory can be seen if we look briefly at one of Lenin's last compositions, "Our Revolution," a reply to N. Sukhanov's condemnation of the Bolshevik revolution. Sukhanov's major point was that Lenin's revolution was premature, that the objective economic conditions for socialism did not exist, nor had the Russian proletariat achieved the necessary level of culture. Lenin's response:

> If a definite level of culture is required for the building of socialism (although nobody can say just what the definite "level of culture" is . . .) why cannot we begin by first achieving the prerequisites for that definite level of culture in a revolutionary way, and *then,* with the aid of the workers' and peasants' government and the Soviet system, proceed to overtake other nations? (*SW,* III, 769)

To this there is a reply. Unless the bulk of the population has attained the "necessary level of culture," they cannot be trusted to rule themselves. Thus the worker and peasant government must, for a lengthy period of reeducation, be a government for these groups but not by them. Until the force of habit is stamped out and the necessary level of culture achieved, Lenin's ideas license dictatorship of the many by the few, for an entire historical era.[35]

Conclusion

As we have noted, Lenin's Jacobin tendencies were criticized by other figures in the socialist movement long before the Bolshevik revolution. Among revolutionary socialists, Lenin's view was distinctive in how little faith he had in historical actors other than himself. He did not trust the bourgeoisie to pursue a revolutionary course and so argued that the revolution had to be made without their support—in fact, in spite of their opposition.[1] We have seen his lack of faith in the working class's ability to develop revolutionary consciousness of their own accord and so the need to combat spontaneity. Bolshevism is impatient Marxism. Lenin always knew his goal; to get there he not only wished to give history a push but also developed the kind of disciplined party that was necessary to do the pushing. But this raises the question of how far Lenin succeeded. More than the abuses of his own relatively brief time in power, under Stalin the regime he had wrought became one of the archtyrannies in human history. It is likely that by the time of his death, Lenin had strong reservations about Soviet society and where it had gotten off track. Much of his failing energy during his last years was spent devising fixes to restore the system's revolutionary soul. But all Lenin's schemes, if implemented at all, were soon subverted by the new existing order.[2]

In spite of the inadequacies of Bakunin's theory, the history of the Soviet Union confirmed his worst fears about revolutionary movements. Ulam relates how Yuri Steklov, Bakunin's Communist biographer, patiently criticized the anarchist's theoretical errors. But then, since Steklov died in a Stalinist concentration camp, one can wonder about his final thoughts on the matter.[3]

During Lenin's lifetime, one of his most trenchant critics was Rosa Luxembourg. A revolutionary socialist in many ways like himself, Luxembourg rejected Lenin's espousal of the relationship between theory and practice. Rather than believe, like Lenin (and Trotsky), that socialism "is something for which a ready-made formula lies completed in the pocket of the revolutionary party," waiting only to be implemented, she insisted that socialism had to be worked out by the masses in the course of revolutionary activity.[4] Like Lenin, she believed that socialism required "a complete spiritual transformation of the masses." But she believed that this could not be effected through Lenin's preferred means, based on authority and terror. What was required was "the most unlimited, the broadest democracy and public opinion."[5]

If Lenin was wrong in believing in his party, Luxembourg erred in the opposite direction. Throughout her life she placed her faith in the revolutionary potential of the masses — dying in 1919 as the result of an abortive uprising in Germany. But although throughout history the masses have risen, the evidence of their commitment to identifiable forms of socialism or other end states is uncertain at best.

Students of revolutions distinguish between what we can call rebellions and revolutions. The former are assaults on existing authority structures; the latter involve "conscious espousal of a new social order," which political actors attempt to realize.[6] The last century witnessed more than a few examples of the latter kind — Russian, Chinese, Vietnamese, Cuban, Iranian, and others. But my subject in this book goes beyond even creation of a new social order. The orders that concern me break more sharply with what exists. Once again, central to the Manuels' definition of utopia is "a new state of being," "a human condition that is totally new by any standard."[7] The societies in question must represent attempts at perfection, of different sorts. They must be without the problems and strife of existing societies. Plato's philosopher-king will allow cities to have "rest from evils" (*Rep.* 473). Robespierre's aspiration is "to fulfil the course of nature, to accomplish the destiny of mankind, to make good the promises of philosophy, to absolve Providence from the long reign of crime and tyranny."[8] Marx sees in Communism the reconciliation of the conflict between existence and essence, the solution to the riddle of history.[9]

Granted distinctions between kinds and levels of political change, questions naturally arise about the applicability of what we have seen throughout this book to less fundamental reform. Although such questions cannot be answered here, they should at least be raised—if only to be set aside. It should be noted that the connections drawn throughout this book are specific. Our subject is fundamental reform. We have seen repeatedly that this requires transformation of people as well as circumstances, creation of a radically new human type, and I have traced the unsettling implications of the political preconditions of intensive education.

What, then, does this imply for less fundamental reform? If creation of the new man requires intensive education, can we assume that less comprehensive reforms require less? The implications of such a conclusion would be important. If less is required of education, associated political problems will be similarly less daunting, and so the main themes of our inquiries would tell less strongly against such efforts. Along similar lines, in our discussion of Plato we encountered Karl Popper's proposed method of reform, piecemeal social engineering (see above, pp. 51–52). Reformers should target obvious evils and then, learning through trial and error, move on to additional problems. The great advantage of this method is that it allows reformers to make tangible improvements in society while also gaining expertise about the techniques of reform, so as to be able to make further positive changes more effectively. As we saw, the great problem with Popper's method is that it never breaks decisively with existing society and so cannot lead to fundamental change. But if fundamental change is not the aim, the method clearly has much to recommend it. And so, obviously, it is important to know how well it can work, including conditions that make it more effective.

However, once again, although such questions are of both theoretical and practical importance, they cannot be explored here. To discuss them adequately would require a work as large as the present one, a task

I cannot undertake. And so my conclusions hold only for fundamental reform, with their wider applicability left open.

To bring this work to a close, let us review the main conclusions. Central to the discussion is educational realism. Creation of the new man requires intensive education. This in turn requires political control and so sets the stage for possible tyranny. These themes are illuminated by the development of Lenin's political thought. In his anarchistic and idyllic *State and Revolution,* Lenin recognizes the need for a new order of human beings; communism "presupposes not the present productivity of labour and *not the present* ordinary run of people" (*SW,* II, 358). But Lenin's postulation is not accompanied by adequate exploration of the means of generating the necessary human types. He confronted this deficiency in the years following the Revolution but in doing so helped to justify unchecked Party control. In regard to these central problems, the thinness of Marxian theory as represented by Marx and Engels is apparent. On one level, Marx has a defensible answer to the question of generating new human beings. In the sixth Thesis on Feuerbach, Marx describes "the human essence" as "the ensemble of the social relations."[10] If people are decisively shaped by their environment, then it follows that, as corrupting conditions have made people corrupt, the purified conditions of the new society can have the desired effects. But this leaves out the question of transition. How do we move from the corrupted individuals of existing society to the new order?

It is important to note that the criticism here does not depend on ultimate, unverifiable claims about human nature. Obviously, if human nature is somehow ineluctably fixed—as in the thought of such theorists as Saint Augustine, Hobbes, and Freud—then attempts to perfect human nature cannot succeed. In contrast, the point here is that even if human nature is capable of change, even of something approaching perfection, we must recognize the demanding measures this will require. The difficulty of the transition does not rest on ultimate assumptions but on easily observed facts of human behavior.

According to educational realism, the transformation will require time and in-depth education. There is little reason to believe that revolution itself will transform human nature. Rather, people must be educated intensively, from their earliest years. If we accept these points, then their political implications must be reckoned with. Education requires control. Especially during the period of transition from the old society to the new, educational authorities must be able to mold the citizenry according to their designs. They must also be able to do so in spite of possible resistance from members of the existing order—who are moved by precisely the desires and dispositions that must be wiped away. In other words, educational authorities must have unchecked political authority.

The problems here are obvious. If educational realism requires unchecked political power, then the possibilities of abuse are apparent. Means must be devised to ensure that educator-rulers do not betray their trust. In the Jacobin tradition, the necessary means appealed to are generally moral. Accordingly, to the six points that constitute Jacobinism, as discussed above, we can add one more:

(J.7) The enlightened minority do not desire to use their power to benefit themselves, but solely for the benefit of their charges.

In the literature we have examined, (J.7) generally depends on the virtue of the rulers—whether the prodigious nature of Plato's philosopher, the great soul of Rousseau's lawgiver, or Bakunin's natural authority. As Robespierre said of virtue in his last speech to the Convention: "You feel it now burning in your souls, just as I feel it in mine."[11] History, however, has shown that this is not an attractive bet. As Machiavelli classically argues, because moral reform presupposes a good man while the means to power presuppose a bad one, a person with the requisite combination of qualities to use for good what he has attained through evil will be exceedingly rare.

We return to the dilemma noted in the last chapter. If the masses must be led—and more, subject to intensive conditioning—then one must confront the leaders' possible abuse of power. Historical attempts to circumvent this dilemma have ended up either ineffectual or corrupted. Either the complacent masses do not rise or they do, following leaders who betray them. Perhaps a successful outcome is not absolutely impossible. Perhaps, as Plato argues, we cannot rule out the possibility that in the fullness of time enlightened revolutionary leaders will arise, who, like Rousseau's lawgiver, are immune from the promptings of human passions. Although

Bakunin believes that rulers will always become corrupt, it is possible that particular rulers will not. It is impossible to prove a negative, and I will not attempt to do so. But even as we leave open this possibility, we cannot but recognize how rare and improbable it is. To return to Plato once again, given the need to remold future subjects and what this requires politically, the radical reformer's hope must be dashed. He is inevitably foredoomed to failure, unless, that is, "some divine good luck chances to be his" (*Rep.* 592a).

Notes

<small>INTRODUCTION</small>

1. F. E. Manuel and F. P. Manuel, *Utopian Thought in the Western World* (Cambridge, Mass., 1979); K. Kumar, *Utopia and Anti-Utopia in Modern Times* (Oxford, 1987); G. Kateb, *Utopia and Its Enemies* (1963; rpt. New York, 1972).

2. Manuel and Manuel, *Utopian Thought*, p. 9.

3. Plutarch, *Lycurgus,* 31; B. Perin, trans., in *Plutarch's Lives* (10 vols.), vol. I (London, 1914). Throughout this work, standard references and abbreviations are used for Classical authors. The latter can be found in Liddell-Scott-Jones, *A Greek-English Lexicon,* various editions.

4. K. Marx, "Theses on Feuerbach," #6, in *Karl Marx and Frederick Engels: Selected Works in Three Volumes,* no trans. (Moscow, 1966), I, 14.

5. S. Freud, *Civilization and Its Discontents,* ed. and trans. J. Strachey (New York, 1961); G. Mosca, *The Ruling Class,* ed. A. Livingston, trans. H. Kahn (New York, 1939).

6. As K. Mannheim argues, ideological concerns are important in regard to where such lines are drawn. *Ideology and Utopia* (New York, 1936), chap. 2.

7. Manuel and Manuel, *Utopian Thought*, both quotes, p. 8.

8. According to Manuel and Manuel, for this the term "uchronia" was invented by the French philosopher Charles Renouvier (*Utopian Thought,* p. 4).

9. Important works that cover different aspects of this subject, from which I have learned a great deal, include K. Popper, *The Open Society and Its Enemies,* vol. I, *The Spell of Plato,* 5th ed. (Princeton, 1966); J. L. Talmon, *The Origins of Totalitarian Democracy* (New York, 1970); and numerous works of Isaiah Berlin, e.g., *Four Essays on Liberty* (Oxford, 1969), *The Crooked Timber of Humanity* (London, 1990), *Against the Current* (1979; rpt. New York, 1982), and *Russian Thinkers* (New York, 1982). Kateb, *Utopia and Its Enemies,* chap. 2, is an excellent general discussion.

Chapter One.   Ancient Lawgivers

1. Aristophanes, *The Birds* 1281–83, trans. D. Barrett; *The Knights, Peace, The Birds, The Assemblywomen, Wealth* (Harmondsworth, 1978).

2. For lives of Lycurgus and Solon, I use the Loeb Classics Library edition, *Plutarch's Lives,* 10 vols., vol. I, trans. B. Perin (London, 1914).

3. W. G. Forrest (*A History of Sparta, 950–192* B.C. [New York, 1969]) argues for the seventh century (pp. 55–58). According to N. G. L. Hammond, modern scholars place Lycurgus anywhere between the late ninth to the sixth century (*A History of Greece to 322* B.C., 2d ed. [Oxford, 1967], p. 103); A. Andrewes (*The Greek Tyrants* [1956; rpt. New York, 1963) argues that seventh-century reforms were attributed to Lycurgus, who was an earlier and by then shadowy figure (pp. 76–77).

4. Andrewes, *Greek Tyrants,* p. 77.

5. Herodotus, 7.225; *The Histories,* trans. A. de Selincourt, rev. ed. (Harmondsworth, 1972).

6. For discussion, see G. Klosko, *History of Political Theory: An Introduction,* vol. I, *Ancient and Medieval Political Theory* (Fort Worth, 1993), pp. 160–65.

7. These remarks recall themes in Plato's political theory; see *Ep.* 7 330c–31b; see below, p. 50.

8. Aristotle, *The Politics,* rev. ed., trans. T. Sinclair and T. Saunders (Harmondsworth, 1981).

9. For discussion of Solon's reforms, see Aristotle, *Constitution of Athens,* 5–14; Hammond, *History of Greece,* 157–63; D. Stockton, *The Classical Athenian Democracy* (Oxford, 1990), chap. 2.

10. *Solon,* 13; see Andrewes, *Greek Tyrants,* on the role of the Greek tyrants in creating the conditions for democracy.

CHAPTER TWO.   SOCRATIC REFORM

1. Brief discussions of these issues, with additional references, are found in G. Klosko, *The Development of Plato's Political Theory* (New York, 1986), chap. 2. For Plato's works, I use J. Burnet, ed., *Platonis Opera,* 5 vols. (Oxford, 1900–1907). For works of Plato and Aristotle, unless indicated otherwise, I use Loeb Classics Library translations, occasionally modified slightly. The exceptions are as follows: for the *Republic,* I use the translation of G. M. A. Grube (Indianapolis, 1974); for the *Laws,* the translation of T. Saunders (Harmondsworth, 1970); for the *Epistles,* the translation of G. Morrow (Indianapolis, 1962). The translation of Thucydides is the Penguin revised edition, translated by R. Warner (Harmondsworth, 1972). I use standard abbreviations for works of Classical authors; these can be found in Liddell and Scott's *Greek-English Lexicon.*

2. Aside from the death of Socrates, in 399, two references are to the King's Peace of 386 in the *Menexenus* (244d–46a) and to the death of Theaetetus in the *Theaetetus.* For discussion, see W. K. C. Guthrie, *A History of Greek Philosophy,* 6 vols. (Cambridge, 1962–81), IV, 52–54.

3. For an excellent, brief discussion of this sort of analysis, see L. Brandwood, "Stylometry and Chronology," in *The Cambridge Companion to Plato,* ed. R. Kraut (Cambridge, 1992).

4. F. M. Cornford, ed. and trans., *The Republic of Plato* (Oxford, 1941), vii–ix.

5. An example is the *Oeconomicus;* for a brief discussion, see Guthrie, *History,* III, 335–38.

6. For the relevant fragments in English translation, see G. C. Field, *Plato and His Contemporaries,* 3d ed. (London, 1967), pp. 147–49. The *Dissoi Logoi* also address several themes discussed by Plato's Socrates.

7. On the proleptic nature of the early dialogues, see W. Jaeger, *Paideia,* trans. G. Highet (Oxford, 1939–45), II, 96; Klosko, *Development,* chap. 2; for a variant of this view, see C. Kahn, *Plato and the Socratic Dialogue* (Cambridge, 1996).

8. Important scholars argue for the historical accuracy of the *Apology,* e.g., C. D. C. Reeve, *Socrates in the Apology* (Indianapolis, 1989); T. Brickhouse and N. Smith, *Socrates on Trial* (Oxford, 1988). I am skeptical, however. The main consideration in favor of historical accuracy is that many of Plato's readers would have heard Socrates' actual speech, so how could Plato depart from it? The obvious problem with this line of argument is the existence of a number of versions of Socrates' speech that differ substantially. Most notably, Xenophon's *Apology* is of course extant and differs appreciably from Plato's. Especially intriguing is the claim of Libanius, in *The Silence of Socrates,* that Socrates was not

allowed to offer a defense and so remained silent. In regard to the speeches he includes in his *History,* Thucydides distinguishes between what the speakers actually said and what they *should have* said, i.e., what the circumstances called for (*ta deonta*) (I, 22). I believe it is likely that the *Apology* is what Plato thought Socrates *should have said,* what the circumstances at his trial called for, rather than the speech he actually made. The hypothesis that authors of various apologies recounted their conceptions of what Socrates should have said would explain the different versions of Socrates' speech.

That Plato's *Apology* is his composition rather than what Socrates actually said is confirmed by the highly literary form of the speech and its close resemblance to Gorgias's *Defense of Palamedes;* see J. Coulter, "The Relation of the *Apology of Socrates* to Gorgias's *Defense of Palamedes* and Plato's Critique of Gorgianic Rhetoric," *Harvard Studies in Classical Philology* 68 (1964); cf. Guthrie, *History,* IV, 76–77. Regardless of the historical accuracy of the speech, however, there is little reason to believe that it does not present an accurate account of the character and teaching of the historical Socrates—as Plato understood him. Regardless of the words Socrates actually used, what the circumstances "called for" was, according to Plato, an overall account of Socrates' mission and teaching, which is what he supplied.

9. In Socrates' thought, "justice" and "virtue" are often interchangeable.

10. For two views of the unity of the virtues, see T. Penner, "The Unity of Virtue," *Philosophical Review* 82 (1973); G. Vlastos, "The Unity of the Virtues in the *Protagoras,*" in *Platonic Studies* (Princeton, 1973).

11. This reconstruction of the argument follows G. Santas, *Socrates: Philosophy in Plato's Early Dialogues* (London, 1979).

12. See also *EE* 1216b5–11. There is controversy on the authenticity of the *Magna Moralia,* which is generally viewed as pseudo-Aristotelian; for references, see Guthrie, *History,* VI, 336n.3; for defense of the authenticity of the work, see J. Cooper, "The *Magna Moralia* and Aristotle's Moral Philosophy," *American Journal of Philology* 94 (1973). Regardless of whether the *MM* is by Aristotle himself, the view it expresses on Socrates' moral views is consistent with that in the *Eudemian* and *Nicomachean Ethics;* the complete evidence of Aristotle is assembled and translated into French, with reasonable commentary, in T. Deman, *Le témoignage d'Aristote sur Socrate* (Paris, 1942).

13. For analysis of the argument, see Klosko, "On the Analysis of Protagoras 351B–360E," *Phoenix* 34 (1980).

14. Aristotle *Rhet.* 1393b5–9; Xenophon *Mem.* 1.2.9; 3.9.10–12.

15. Guthrie, *History,* III, 411–16.

16. *Ap.* 28d–e; *Symp.* 220d–21c; *Lach.* 181b.

17. J. Burnet, "The Socratic Doctrine of the Soul," *Proceedings of the British Academy* 7 (1915 – 16): 238 – 40.

18. This is even more true in Xenophon's *Memorabilia*. See, e.g., the discussions with Pistias the armor maker and Theodote the courtesan (III, 10 and 11). Depiction of such interlocutors in Plato as well as Xenophon indicates the hollowness of the claim that the *elenchos* is primarily a positive method for establishing philosophical propositions; see Vlastos, "The Socratic Elenchus," *Oxford Studies in Ancient Philosophy* 1 (1983). If Socrates' motivation had been primarily philosophical, after many years he would clearly have recognized how little he had to learn from characters such as Euthyphro and would have confined his attention to people more worth talking to.

19. Although there is no real evidence for this, it is tempting to infer a relationship between Socrates' view and the idea of the city of the virtuous, a city without institutions, that was later expounded by Zeno of Citium, the founder of Stoicism; see Diogenes Laertius VII, 33 – 34. This connection is made by Cornford, "Plato's Commonwealth," in *The Unwritten Philosophy and Other Essays,* ed. W. K. C. Guthrie (Cambridge, 1950), p. 60.

20. I view the *Alcibiades I* as genuine (see below, p. 41). For a brief discussion with numerous references, see P. Friedlander, *Plato,* trans. H. Meyerhoff (Princeton, 1958 – 69), vol. II, chap. 17.

21. The encounters between Socrates and his interlocutors described below are discussed in detail in Klosko, "The Politics of Philosophy: The Origin and Development of Plato's Political Theory" (Ph. D. dissertation, Columbia University, 1977). Discussion here draws on Klosko, "Rational Persuasion in Plato's Political Theory," *History of Political Thought* 7 (1986); and "The Insufficiency of Reason in Plato's *Gorgias,*" *Western Political Quarterly* 36 (1983). Criteria that can be used to assess whether the relationship between the characters in a given dialogue is able to satisfy the necessary conditions for a successful *elenchos* are discussed in *The Politics of Philosophy* and "Insufficiency of Reason."

22. For the playful threat of force, repeatedly voiced by Protarchus, see *Phil.* 19d – e, 23b, 50d – e, 67b.

23. On Anytus, see R. S. Bluck, *Plato's Meno* (Cambridge, 1961), pp. 126 – 28.

24. Friedlander, *Plato,* II, 233 – 34.

25. The *Alcibiades I* is situated in about 433, when Socrates was about thirty-seven and Alcibiades about fifteen years old (Friedlander, *Plato,* II, 232). The banquet in honor of Agathon's victory — and so the *Symposium* — took place in 416 or 415 (Guthrie, *History,* IV, 365 – 66), when Socrates was about fifty-five and Alcibiades about thirty-three. For Alcibiades at this stage of his life, see, esp. Thucydides, VI, 12 – 18.

26. See Klosko, "Insufficiency of Reason."

27. For the *Gorgias* anticipating the political theory of the *Republic,* see E. Barker, *Greek Political Theory: Plato and His Predecessors* (London, 1947), pp. 165–67; M. Pohlenz, *Aus Platos Werdezeit* (Berlin, 1913), pp. 152–64; T. Irwin, ed., *Plato: Gorgias* (Oxford, 1979), p. 215.

28. Although Socrates is not mentioned by name here, it is likely that he is the target of Aristotle's remarks; see N. Gulley, *The Philosophy of Socrates* (London, 1968), pp. 135–38.

29. For an account of Plato's conception of virtue in the *Republic* and other middle dialogues, see Klosko, *Development,* pt. II; and "The 'Rule' of Reason in Plato's Psychology," *History of Philosophy Quarterly* 5 (1988). Many scholars argue that the conception of virtue in the *Republic* represents the decisive repudiation of Socrates' intellectualism; see, e.g., Irwin, *Plato's Moral Theory* (Oxford, 1977), pp. 191–216; Pohlenz, *Aus Platos Werdezeit,* 156–57. There is strong evidence that some version of Plato's more mature psychology is present in the *Gorgias;* see Irwin, *Gorgias,* notes on 491d4, 493a, 499e–500a, 505bc, 507ab.

30. J. Gould, *The Development of Plato's Ethics* (New York, 1972).

31. See above, n. 29.

CHAPTER THREE.   THE POLITICS OF PHILOSOPHY

1. *Spirit of the Laws,* bk. 19, chap. 4.

2. K. Popper, *The Open Society and Its Enemies,* vol. I, *The Spell of Plato,* 5th ed. (Princeton, 1966); Popper's account of Plato is analyzed in G. Klosko, "Popper's Plato: An Assessment," *Philosophy of the Social Sciences* 26 (1996).

3. Popper, *Open Society,* chap. 9.

4. See Klosko, "Provisionality in Plato's Ideal State," *History of Political Thought* 5 (1984).

5. See *Statesman* 293d–e, 296d–e; for a brief discussion, see G. Klosko, *The Development of Plato's Political Theory* (New York, 1986), pp. 188–94.

6. For example, Dion's taking power by violence was perhaps justified as falling under exceptional circumstances, because Dionysius II was a tyrant. The violence of the ruler in the *Statesman* is perhaps justified because, as the discussion indicates, he is a legitimate ruler, and so the question of his taking power does not arise. However, the argument in the *Statesman* is that knowledge alone makes one legitimate, without reference to sources of political power. Unless the philosopher's city is a tyranny, neither of these circumstances obtains in his case.

It is difficult to say how deeply Plato was involved in Dion's plans. In *Epistle 7,* Plato says that he opposed Dion's invasion (350c–e). But since the epistle was written in the aftermath of the invasion and its unfortunate fallout, from which Plato wished to dissociate himself, it is not clear how much stock can be put in this account. For a good discussion of Plato and Dion, see G. Morrow, ed. and trans., *Plato: Epistles,* rev. ed. (Indianapolis, 1962), pp. 118–80.

7. Cf. Klosko, *Development,* p. 179, which is incorrect in presenting a conventional interpretation of the passage.

8. For discussion, see Klosko, *Development,* pp. 238–40.

9. Ibid., pp. 238–39.

10. J. Burnet, *Greek Philosophy: Part I, Thales to Plato* (London, 1914), pp. 295, 300; W. K. C. Guthrie, *A History of Greek Philosophy,* 6 vols. (Cambridge, 1962–81), IV, 29.

11. E. Barker, *Greek Political Theory: Plato and His Predecessors* (London, 1918; rpt. 1947), pp. 277–78.

12. R. L. Nettleship, *Lectures on the Republic of Plato,* 2d ed. (London, 1901), p. 211; F. M. Cornford, *The Republic of Plato* (Oxford, 1941), xxv; F. M. Cornford, *Plato's Cosmology* (1937; rpt. Indianapolis, 1957), p. 5; T. A. Sinclair, *A History of Greek Political Thought,* 2d ed. (Cleveland, 1967), pp. 157–59; H. Raeder, *Platons Philosophische Entwickelung* (Leipzig, 1905), p. 222.

13. It seems to me possible that, since Popper and other scholars called attention to unpleasant aspects of Plato's *Republic* in *Open Society* and other works, Plato's supporters have had an incentive to downplay the extent to which the work is seriously intended, much as some Nietzsche scholars denied that Nietzsche had a political theory, in the years after World War II, when Nietzsche had been branded a proto-Nazi; see W. Kaufmann, *Nietzsche: Philosopher, Psychologist, Antichrist,* 4th ed. (Princeton, 1974); for discussion, see B. Detweiler, *Nietzsche and the Politics of Aristocratic Radicalism* (Chicago, 1990), pp. 3, 37–44. A moderate view, that Plato wavers on questions of political reform, is presented by J. Annas, *An Introduction to Plato's Republic* (Oxford, 1981), pp. 185–87.

14. Guthrie, *History,* IV, 470 (his emphasis); see also 434 and n. 2. Similar positions are held by I. M. Crombie, *An Examination of Plato's Doctrines,* 2 vols. (London, 1962–63), I, 131; R. D. Levinson, *In Defense of Plato* (Cambridge, Mass., 1953), pp. 573–76.

15. See E. R. Dodds, *Plato: Gorgias* (Oxford, 1959), pp. 1–5.

16. Annas, *Introduction,* p. 171; Annas is here referring to *Rep.* 449a–71e.

17. This point made by R. Demos, "Paradoxes in Plato's Doctrine of the Idea State," *Classical Quarterly* N. S. 7 (1957): 169.

18. Crombie, *Examination,* I, 131; Levinson, *Defense,* p. 348; also A. Bloom, *The Republic of Plato* (New York: Basic Books, 1968), p. 409.

19. Bloom, *Republic,* p. 410.

20. L. Strauss, *The City and Man* (Chicago, 1963), p. 65.

21. For discussion of additional problems with their method, see G. Klosko, "The 'Straussian' Interpretation of Plato's *Republic,*" *History of Political Thought* 7 (1986): 278–79. This article covers many of the issues discussed below in greater detail; I draw on it in several contexts here.

22. Bloom, *Republic,* xviii; for further references, see Klosko, "Straussian Interpretation," 279 n.13.

23. L. Bloom, "A Response to Hall," *Political Theory* 5 (1977). I will not discuss the purported absurdity of making the philosophers rule. The absurdity, it has been claimed, is because of the injustice to the philosophers that this represents. See Bloom, *Republic,* pp. 407–10; Strauss, *City and Man,* p. 124; for discussion, see Klosko, "Straussian Interpretation," 290–92; G. Klosko, "Implementing the Ideal State," *Journal of Politics* 43 (1981): 370.

24. Bloom, "Response," p. 324.

25. Ibid.

26. Bloom, *Republic,* pp. 385–87; similarly Strauss, *City and Man,* pp. 116–17.

27. For discussion of the fact that in the *Republic* Plato actually recognizes the legitimacy of the body and its desires, in comparison, for example, to the argument of the *Phaedo,* see Klosko, "Straussian Interpretation," p. 289, which contains additional references.

28. For discussion of another of Strauss's and Bloom's arguments, that the *Republic* is some sort of parody of Aristophanes' *Ecclesiazusae,* see Klosko, "Straussian Interpretation," 282–87.

29. For the date of the *Republic,* see Guthrie, *History,* IV, 437, with many references; for the date of *Epistle* 7, see Morrow, *Epistles,* p. 45.

30. For discussion of the authenticity of *Epistle* 7, see Morrow, *Epistles,* pp. 44–81; Guthrie, *History,* V, 399–401; cf. M. Schofield, "Plato and Practical Politics," in *The Cambridge History of Greek and Roman Political Thought,* ed. M. Schofield and C. Rowe (Cambridge, 2000), pp. 298–302.

31. See P. M. Schuhl, "Platon et l'activité politique de l'academie," *Revue des Etudes Grecques* 59 (1946). See below, n. 33.

32. Morrow, *Epistles,* p. 143.

33. Ibid., pp. 173–74. For contrary views of the evidence, see P. A. Brunt, *Studies in Greek History and Thought* (Oxford, 1993), chap. 10; Schofield, "Plato and Practical Politics." In spite of the doubts these and other scholars raise about various specific pieces of evidence, there can be no doubt about Aris-

totle's tutoring Alexander of Macedon, Dion's invasion of Sicily, and the involvement of the Academy in Dion's invasion.

34. Morrow, *Epistles,* p. 144; K. von Fritz, *Pythagorean Politics in Southern Italy* (1940; rpt. New York, 1977)

35. See Klosko, *Development,* pp. 59–63.

36. D. L. VIII, 79; see Guthrie, *History,* I, 333–36.

37. Aristotle, *Art of Rhetoric,* trans. J. H. Freese (Cambridge, Mass., 1926).

CHAPTER FOUR.   THREE THEORISTS OF REFORM

1. T. More, *Utopia,* trans. P. Turner (Harmondsworth, 1965), p. 84; this work is cited hereafter in the text.

2. Quoted by K. Kumar, *Utopia and Anti-Utopia in Modern Times* (Oxford, 1987), p. 430 n.60.

3. F. E. Manuel and F. P. Manuel, *Utopian Thought in the Western World* (Cambridge, Mass., 1979), p. 135.

4. J. H. Hexter, *More's Utopia: The Biography of an Idea* (Princeton, 1952).

5. This is shown, for example, in Machiavelli's opposition to the use of artillery, in *Discourse,* II, 17.

6. Machiavelli is quoted from *Machiavelli: The Chief Works and Others,* trans. A. Gilbert, 3 vols. (Durham, N. C., 1965). The *Discourses* is cited as *Dis.,* by book and chapter number and by page number in this edition; and the *Prince,* by chapter number and page number in this edition. For both works, all page references are to volume I.

7. As Rousseau points out in his *Discourse on Political Economy; Jean-Jacques Rousseau: Basic Political Writings,* trans. D. Cress (Indianapolis, 1987), p. 126.

8. J. W. Allen, *A History of Political Thought in the Sixteenth Century* (London, 1928), p. 478.

9. *Dis.,* I, 2; I, 9; for the historicity of Lycurgus, see above, chap. 2. As J. G. A. Pocock notes (*The Machiavellian Moment* [Princeton, 1975], p. 168), Lycurgus and Solon are not included in Machiavelli's list of state founders in chapter 6 of the *Prince,* as Machiavelli viewed them as reformers rather than creators of states.

10. J. Shklar, *Men and Citizens* (Cambridge, 1985), p. vii.

11. J.-J. Rousseau, *Emile,* trans. B. Foxley (London, 1911), pp. 422–23. Rousseau's *Social Contract* is quoted from *Jean-Jacques Rousseau: The Basic Political Writings,* trans. D. Cress (Indianapolis, 1987); this is abbreviated *S. C.* in the text and cited by book and chapter numbers and by page numbers in this edition.

12. For discussion, see Pocock, *Machiavellian Moment,* chap. 7. This is not a subject that Machiavelli pursues systematically or in detail. But in another respect Machiavelli considers a central precondition—a political precondition—for radical reform. For a people to be receptive to a reformer's message, they must be in distress; see esp. *Prince,* chap. 26.

13. Matteo Buttafuco, letter to Rousseau; quoted in C. Vaughan, ed., *The Political Writings of Jean Jacques Rousseau,* 2 vols. (1915; rpt. New York, 1962), II, 293. For Rousseau's *Constitutional Project for Corsica,* I use the translation in *Jean-Jacques Rousseau: Political Writings,* trans. F. Watkins (1953; rpt. Madison, Wis., 1986) (referred to in the text as *Corsica*). For *The Government of Poland,* I use the translation by Wilmoore Kendall (Indianapolis, 1972) (referred to in the text as *Poland*).

14. Quoted by M. Cranston, *The Solitary Self: Jean-Jacques Rousseau in Exile and Adversity* (Chicago, 1997), p. 94.

15. Vaughan, *Political Writings,* II, 295; for discussion, see II, 293–305.

16. Quoted in Vaughan, *Political Writings,* II, 297; this is a fragment, disconnected from the text of the work as a whole.

17. Vaughan, *Political Writings,* II, 298.

18. Cranston, *Solitary Self,* p. 141.

19. Ibid., p. 177; on conditions in Poland, see Vaughan, *Political Writings,* II, 376–90.

20. Cranston, *Solitary Self,* p. 179.

CHAPTER FIVE.   THE JACOBIN IDEAL

1. K. Popper, *The Open Society and Its Enemies,* vol. I, *The Spell of Plato,* 5th ed. (Princeton, 1966), chap. 3.

2. For discussion, see G. Klosko, *History of Political Theory: An Introduction,* vol. II, *Modern Political Theory* (Fort Worth, 1995), pp. 23–28.

3. T. More, *Utopia,* trans. P. Turner (Harmondsworth, 1965), pp. 109–17.

4. T. Skocpol, *States and Social Revolutions* (Cambridge, 1979).

5. K. Popper, *Conjectures and Refutations: The Growth of Scientific Knowledge* (New York, 1963), p. 358; cf. Popper, *Open Society,* chap. 9: "Aestheticism, Perfectionism. Utopianism."

6. C. Brinton, *The Jacobins* (New York, 1930), p. 39; cf. the figures presented by P. Higonnet, *Goodness beyond Virtue: Jacobins during the French Revolution* (Cambridge, Mass., 1998), pp. 48–51, 104.

7. The figure 500,000 is widely accepted, e.g., by R. R. Palmer, *Twelve Who Ruled* (Princeton, 1941), p. 25; for more recent, lower estimates, see Higonnet, *Goodness beyond Virtue,* p. 337 n. 4.

8. Lord Acton, *Lectures on the French Revolution* (New York, 1959), p. 300; T. Carlyle, *The French Revolution* (London, 1906), p. 626.

9. A. Mathiez, *Etudes sur Robespierre* (Paris, 1958; rpt. 1988).

10. N. Hampson, *The Life and Opinions of Maximilien Robespierre* (Oxford, 1974).

11. Robespierre is quoted from his *Oeuvres complètes,* 10 vols. (Paris, 1912–67), cited in the text as *Oeuvres.* There is no satisfactory collection of Robespierre's speeches in English translation; unless otherwise indicated, all translations are my own, although I draw on published translations, especially those in G. Rude, ed., *Robespierre* (Englewood Cliffs, N.J., 1967).

12. An excellent account of the main themes in Robespierre's political thought, and respects in which they developed and remained constant, to which I am indebted, is A. Cobban, *Aspects of the French Revolution* (New York, 1968), chaps. 8, 9.

13. Mathiez, *Etudes,* p. 36; on Robespierre's appearance and voice, see J. Thompson, *Robespierre* (Oxford, 1988), pp. 20–21, 104–5, 585–86.

14. However, as Palmer notes (*Twelve Who Ruled,* p. 272), in their social democratic interpretations of Robespierre, A. Aulard and Mathiez virtually ignore the great speech of February 5, which Palmer characterizes as not only "the most memorable of all Robespierre's speeches" (p. 272) but "the best expressions of Robespierre's real ideas" (p. 275).

15. For Saint-Just's originality as a political thinker, see M. Abensour, "La philosophie politique de Saint-Just," *Annales Historiques de la Révolution Française* 183 (1966). Two valuable recent studies of Jacobin ideas are Higgonet, *Goodness beyond Virtue,* and C. Blum, *Rousseau and the Republic of Virtue* (Ithaca, 1986).

16. See Cobban, *Aspects,* chaps. 8, 9. This work is cited in the text as Cobban; translations of French quotations are mine.

17. See Thompson, *Robespierre,* chap. 7.

18. This translation draws from Palmer, *Twelve Who Ruled,* pp. 275–77.

19. The circumstances in the Year II and policies the Committee of Public Safety took to meet them are discussed in highly readable form in Palmer, *Twelve Who Ruled.*

20. For support for this interpretation, see Mathiez, *Etudes.*

21. Quoted in N. Hampson, *Will and Circumstance* (London, 1983), p. 229.

22. Thompson, *Robespierre,* pp. 315–16, 323.

23. *Papiers inédits trouvés chez Robespierre, Saint-Just, Payan, etc.,* 3 vols. (Paris, 1828), II, 13.

24. It should be noted that *terreur* can be translated as "intimidation" as much as "terror" (Thompson, *Robespierre,* p. 452 n. 1).

25. The text of the law is reprinted in J. Thompson, *French Revolution: Documents, 1789–94* (Oxford, 1933), pp. 284–87. For discussion, see J. Thompson, *The French Revolution* (1943; rpt. New York, 1966), pp. 535–36; Palmer, *Twelve Who Ruled,* pp. 364–66.

26. Thompson, *Robespierre,* p. 515.

27. Ibid., pp. 505–11.

28. *Saint-Just: Oeuvres Complètes,* ed. Michele Duval (Paris, 1984), p. 778. Saint-Just's works are cited below as *Oeuvres;* all translations are mine.

29. For discussion, see H. C. Barnard, *Education and the French Revolution* (Cambridge, 1969), pp. 118–23.

30. Translation of this speech, with slight modifications, from B. K. Reynolds, ed., *Spokesman of the French Revolution* (New York, 1974), pp. 147–67.

31. Quoted in Blum, *Rousseau and the Republic of Virtue,* p. 246.

32. Quoted in Blum, *Rousseau and the Republic of Virtue,* p. 247.

33. Palmer, *Twelve Who Ruled,* pp. 328–31.

34. Ibid., p. 329.

35. E. N. Curtis, *Saint Just: Colleague of Robespierre* (New York, 1935), p. 211.

36. N. Hampson, *Saint-Just* (Oxford, 1991), p. 229.

37. Maurice Dommanget, "Saint-Just et l'éducation," in *Actes du Colloque Saint-Just,* ed. A. Soboul (Paris, 1968).

38. Curtis, *Saint-Just,* p. 300.

39. As Hampson points out: *Saint-Just,* p. 233.

40. H. J. Parker, *The Cult of Antiquity and the French Revolutionaries* (Chicago, 1937), pp. 159–61.

41. P. Rolland, "La signification politique de l'amitié chez Saint-Just," *Annales Historiques de la Révolution Française* 257 (1984).

42. Hampson, *Saint-Just,* pp. 231–32.

43. F. E. Manuel and F. P. Manuel, *Utopian Thought in the Western World* (Cambridge, Mass., 1979), p. 566.

44. Hampson, *Saint-Just,* p. 235.

45. C. Brinton, "The Political Ideas of St. Just," *Political* (1934): 49–50.

46. Manuel and Manuel, *Utopian Thought,* p. 567.

CHAPTER SIX. THE MARXIAN ALTERNATIVE

1. F. Engels, Letter to W. Borgius, January 25, 1894; in *Marx-Engels: Selected Correspondence,* ed. S. W. Ryazanskaya, trans. I. Lasker, 3d ed. (Moscow, 1975), pp. 441–42. Various themes in this chapter are discussed in more detail in the chapter on Marx in G. Klosko, *History of Political Theory: An Introduction,* vol. II (Fort Worth, 1995), chap. 10, from which some language used here is drawn.

2. K. Marx, *Capital,* 3 vols., ed. F. Engels, trans. S. Moore and E. Aveling (New York, 1967), I, 10 (cited hereafter in the text). In this chapter many works of Marx and Engels are quoted from *Karl Marx and Frederick Engels: Selected Works in Three Volumes,* no trans. (Moscow, 1966), cited in the text as *Works; The Marx-Engels Reader,* 2d ed., ed. R. Tucker (New York, 1978), cited as "Tucker." *The Letters of Karl Marx,* ed. and trans. S. Padover (Englewood Cliffs, N.J., 1979), is cited as *Letters.* Other texts used are cited individually; all italics in quotations from Marx and Engels are theirs.

3. For an exhaustive account of Marx's view of revolutionary change throughout his life, see R. Hunt, *The Political Ideas of Marx and Engels,* 2 vols. (Pittsburgh, 1974, 1985). Hunt's essentially social democratic interpretation of Marx is supported by S. Avineri, *The Social and Political Thought of Karl Marx* (Cambridge, 1968). An important text is Marx's Amsterdam speech of September 8, 1872 (*Works,* I, 292–94). Opposed views are presented in works of Soviet Communism, notably those of Lenin, as discussed in the next chapter. See also J. Talmon, *Political Messianism: The Romantic Phase* (New York, 1960); A. Gilbert, *Marx's Politics: Communists and Citizens* (New Brunswick, N.J., 1981).

4. On Blanqui, see A. B. Spitzer, *The Revolutionary Theories of Louis-Auguste Blanqui* (New York, 1957); G. Lichtheim, *The Origins of Socialism* (New York, 1969), chap. 4.

5. Lichtheim, *Origins of Socialism,* p. 30.

6. J. Beecher, *Charles Fourier: The Visionary and His World* (Berkeley, 1986), p. 23.

7. J. Beecher and R. Bienvenu, eds., *The Utopian Vision of Charles Fourier: Selected Texts on Work, Love, and Passionate Attraction* (Boston, 1971), pp. 116–19. This work is cited in the text as *UV.*

8. Fourier, quoted by N. Riasnovsky, *The Teaching of Charles Fourier* (Berkeley, 1969,) p. 215.

9. Ibid., pp. 217–18.

10. F. E. Manuel and F. P. Manuel, *Utopian Thought in the Western World* (Cambridge, Mass., 1979), p. 642.

11. Beecher, *Charles Fourier,* p. 7.

12. A. Brisbane, ed. and trans., *Charles Fourier: Theory of Social Organization* (New York, 1876), p. 10.

13. Manuel and Manuel, *Utopian Thought,* p. 646.

14. C. Gide, ed., *Design for Utopia: Selected Writings of Charles Fourier* (1901; rpt. New York, 1971), p. 13.

15. See Manuel and Manuel, *Utopian Thought,* pp. 648–49.

16. C. Guarneri, *The Utopian Alternative: Fourierism in Nineteenth-Century America* (Ithaca, 1991), pp. 2–3.

17. Manuel and Manuel, *Utopian Thought,* p. 649.

18. Quoted in Manuel and Manuel, *Utopian Thought,* p. 647.

19. For Fourier's views concerning the need for a legislator, see Gide, ed., *Design for Utopia,* pp. 21–2n.

20. See D. McLellan, *Karl Marx: His Life and Thought* (New York, 1973), chaps. 3, 4; Hunt, *Political Ideas,* I, chaps. 7, 10.

21. Marx, quoted in Hunt, *Political Ideas,* I, 252.

22. Hunt, *Political Ideas,* I, 341.

23. V. I. Lenin, *State and Revolution,* in *Selected Works,* 3 vols. (Moscow, 1970), II, 311.

24. Hunt, *Political Ideas,* I, 297; see chap. 9.

25. As Lenin argues in *State and Revolution,* chaps. 1 and 5.

26. See above, n. 3. Especially notable is Engels's explication of the phrase winning "the battle of democracy," in the *Communist Manifesto* (*Works,* I, 126) as "the winning of universal suffrage, of democracy" (*Works,* I, 195); for discussion, see Hunt, *Political Ideas,* I, 134–38. For similar themes in the thought of Karl Kautsky, see G. Lichtheim, *Marxism: An Historical and Critical Study* (New York, 1961), pp. 270–71.

27. This is one of the main conclusions of Hunt, *Political Ideas.*

28. E. Bernstein, *The Preconditions of Socialism,* ed. and trans. H. Tudor (Cambridge, 1993), p. 158; see chap. 4.

29. Many of these are collected and analyzed in Lenin's *State and Revolution.*

Chapter Seven.   Leninism as Jacobinism

1. This set of options is presented by A. Ulam, *The Bolsheviks* (New York, 1965), p. 74.

2. Lavrov, quoted in Ulam, *Bolsheviks,* p. 73.

3. Ulam, *Bolsheviks,* pp. 83–85; L. Schapiro, *The Communist Party of the Soviet Union,* 2d ed. (New York, 1971), p. 4; R. Theen, *Lenin: Genesis and Development of a Revolutionary* (New York, 1973), pp. 71–76. On use of the term "Jacobin" in the Russian radical tradition, see R. Mayer, "Lenin and the Jacobin Identity in Russia," *Studies in East European Thought* 51 (1999).

4. Quoted in A. Ulam, *In the Name of the People* (New York, 1977), p. 353; emphasis in original. All emphases in quotations in this chapter appear in the original sources, unless otherwise indicated.

5. "Die Lust der Zerstörung is zugleich eine schaffende Lust." Quoted in Paul Thomas, *Karl Marx and the Anarchists* (London, 1980), p. 289.

6. Quoted in E. H. Carr, *Michael Bakunin* (1937; rpt. New York, 1961), p. 254.

7. Bakunin is cited in the text as follows: *God and the State,* no trans. (New York, 1970) (*GS*); *Statism and Anarchy,* ed. and trans. M. Shatz (Cambridge, 1990) (*SA*); *Bakunin on Violence: Letter to S. Nechayev* (New York, n.d.) (*OV*).

8. K. Marx, in *The Marx-Engels Reader,* 2d ed. (New York, 1978), p. 543.

9. Thomas, *Marx and the Anarchists,* p. 286.

10. Bakunin, "The Organization of the International," in *The Basic Bakunin: Writings, 1869–1871,* ed. and trans. R. M. Cutler (Buffalo, 1992), p. 139.

11. For Stenka Razin and Pugachev, see P. Avrich, *Russian Rebels, 1600–1800* (New York, 1972).

12. Quoted in B. Knei-Paz, *The Social and Political Thought of Leon Trotsky* (Oxford, 1978), p. 201; see pp. 199–206.

13. Lenin is quoted from *Lenin: Selected Works in Three Volumes* (Moscow, 1970) (cited in the text as *SW*).

14. See esp. *What Is to Be Done?* Part I: "Dogmatism and 'Freedom of Criticism,'" *SW,* I, 124–41.

15. R. Mayer, "The Status of a Classic Text: Lenin's *What Is to Be Done?* After 1902," *History of European Ideas* 22 (1996).

16. "The overthrow of the bourgeoisie can be achieved only by the proletariat becoming the *ruling class,* capable of crushing the inevitable and desperate resistance of the bourgeoisie, and of organising *all* the working and exploited people for the new economic system" (*SW,* II, 304).

17. N. Harding, *Lenin's Political Thought,* 2 vols. (in one) (1977, 1981; rpt. Atlantic Highlands, N.J., 1983). Similarly, R. Service, *Lenin: A Political Life,* 3 vols. (London and Bloomington, Ind., 1985–95), II, 223, 300–301. It should be noted that even what I take to be the standard position that Lenin breaks with the radicalism of *State and Revolution* within a few weeks of seizing power implies that he adhered to *State and Revolution*'s ideas in the beginning stages

of the Revolution. Schapiro puts this period at about six months (*Communist Party,* pp. 209–10); according to Ulam, it lasted "a few weeks" (*Bolsheviks,* p. 458); see also L. Kolakowski, *Main Currents of Marxism,* 3 vols. (Oxford, 1978) II, 485–86. On this issue, Harding differs from these scholars mainly in asserting that the radical period lasted longer than a few weeks and was based on a deeper commitment to *State and Revolution.*

18. Harding, *Lenin's Political Thought,* II, 178; in discussing Lenin's radicalism, I am indebted to Harding.

19. See "To the Population," *SW,* II, 488–89; "Report on the Economic Conditions of Petrograd Workers," *SW,* II, 505.

20. See Schapiro, *Communist Party,* pp. 161–234: M. Fainsod, *How Russia Is Ruled* (Cambridge, 1953), pp. 124–33.

21. For discussion of this point, I am indebted to Robert Mayer.

22. See esp. *Two Tactics of Social Democracy in the Democratic Revolution* (in *SW,* I).

23. Ulam, *Bolsheviks,* p. 449.

24. Ibid., p. 456.

25. See Harding, *Lenin's Political Thought,* I, chap. 4; H. Willetts, "Lenin and the Peasants," in *Lenin: The Man, the Theorist, the Leader,* ed. L. Schapiro and P. Reddaway (New York, 1967).

26. For the need for the proletariat to lead the peasants in Lenin's earlier writings, see Harding, *Lenin's Political Thought,* I, 100–108.

27. Ibid., II, 188. The positive function is seen also in Lenin's address to the Seventh Party Congress, which is quoted for its radicalism, above: "Soviet power is a new type of state without a bureaucracy, without police, without a regular army, a state in which bourgeois democracy has been replaced by a new democracy, a democracy that brings to the fore the vanguard of the working people, gives them legislative and executive authority, makes them responsible for military defence and creates a state machinery that can re-educate the masses" (*SW,* II, 611).

28. Also: "As I have had occasion to point out more than once . . . the dictatorship of the proletariat is not only the use of force against the exploiter, and not even mainly the use of force. The economic foundation of this use of revolutionary force, the guarantee of its effectiveness and success is the fact that the proletariat represents and creates a higher type of social organization" (III, 230).

29. See also "The Immediate Tasks of the Soviet Government," written between April and May 1918, esp. *SW,* II, 671–73.

30. *SW,* III, 368–69; this is a common theme; see, e.g., "The Tasks of the Youth Leagues," III, 478 (written in October 1920).

31. See, e.g., *SW*, II, 668; see also *The Proletarian Revolution and the Rene-gade Kautsky,* passim.

32. "Report on Party Program, Eighth Congress of the RCP(B)."

33. See, e.g., *"Left Wing" Communism,* where Lenin says that the vanguard "represent[s] the interests of the really foremost and really revolutionary class" (*SW*, III, 410) and that it expresses the "class consciousness, will, passion and imagination" of many millions; see also *SW*, III, 217–18; and A. G. Meyer, *Leninism* (Cambridge, Mass., 1952), p. 208. The position that the Party has a right to rule because it represents the real interests of society — "dictatorship of the idea of the proletariat," as Otto Bauer called it (Meyer, 313 n. 36) was not explicitly formulated until the time of Stalin; see Fainsod, *How Russia Is Ruled,* pp. 127–28, for references.

34. A. Lunacharsky, *On Education: Selected Articles and Speeches,* trans. R. English (Moscow, 1981); in the remainder of this paragraph, references to this edition are given in parentheses in the text.

35. This is stated clearly by J. Stalin, *Foundations of Leninism,* no trans. (New York, 1939), chap. 4.

CONCLUSION

1. V. I. Lenin, *Selected Works in Three Volumes* (Moscow, 1970), I, 151 (cited in the text as *SW*).

2. For a good account, see A. Ulam, *The Bolsheviks* (New York, 1965), chap. 10.

3. Ulam, *Bolsheviks,* p. 41.

4. R. Luxembourg, *The Russian Revolution and Leninism or Marxism,* no trans. (Ann Arbor, 1961), p. 69.

5. Ibid., p. 71.

6. C. Johnson, *Revolutionary Change* (Boston, 1966), pp. 136–38.

7. F. E. Manuel and F. P. Manuel, *Utopian Thought in the Western World* (Cambridge, Mass., 1979), p. 8.

8. M. Robespierre, *Oeuvres Complètes,* 10 vols. (Paris, 1912–67), X, 352.

9. K. Marx, in *The Marx-Engels Reader,* 2d ed., ed. R. Tucker (New York, 1978), p. 84.

10. K. Marx in *Karl Marx and Frederick Engels: Selected Works in Three Volumes,* no trans. (Moscow, 1966), I, 14.

11. Robespierre, *Oeuvres,* X, 554.

Index